The Secrets of
SUCCESSFUL
STAFF APPRAISAL AND
COUNSELLING

The Secrets of

SUCCESSFUL STAFF APPRAISAL AND COUNSELLING

Clive Goodworth

HEINEMANN PROFESSIONAL PUBLISHING

1038053· 1

Dedicated with loving affection to Myra, Paul, Mark, Carl and Anna-Jane Goodworth, who, like most of us, have all suffered the slings and arrows of outrageous appraisal at some time during their working lives. Nil desperandum!

Heinemann Professional Publishing Ltd
Halley Court, Jordan Hill, Oxford OX2 8EJ

OXFORD LONDON MELBOURNE AUCKLAND SINGAPORE
IBADAN NAIROBI GABORONE KINGSTON

First published 1989

© Clive Goodworth 1989

British Library Cataloguing in Publication Data
Goodworth, Clive T.
The secrets of successful staff appraisal and counselling.
1. Personnel. Performance. Assessment
I. Title II. Series
658.3'125
ISBN 0 434 90701 4

Photoset by Deltatype, Ellesmere Port
Printed in Great Britain by Billings of Worcester Ltd

Contents

Figures

Preface

More often than not, the mere mention of staff appraisal is sufficient to set Jack or Jill Manager's teeth on edge; for, let's face it, it's hard to think of any other people-process that's more akin to having an unexploded bomb in one's executive backyard. However, like it or not, appraisal is here to stay, and the purpose of this book is to demonstrate that, provided one treads warily and wisely through the jungle, it can pay handsome dividends. But, *caveat emptor*, cock a snook at Murphy's Law, and, if your luck's anything like mine, it'll all blow up in your face. Which, come to think of it, is one hell of a way to kick off any subject . . .

Welcome aboard, it's time to get cracking!

1 There's nothing new under the sun

When Darius the Great occupied the Persian throne during the fifth century BC, he laboured mightily at the task of introducing new schemes into his government, and – surprise, surprise – one of them was concerned with staff appraisal. It happened this way. Having carved his empire into handy chunks, the worthy monarch had hardly got over the complications of selecting governors to administer them when he suddenly realized that it would be a good idea to keep tabs on their performance. So, setting to with a right royal will, Darius appointed a bevy of appraisers (oh, all right, secret police), whose job it was to submit regular, formal assessments on the strengths, weaknesses and sundry capers of these well-paid gaffers. And true to the fashion of those good old days, it wasn't long before their reported failings had the executioner's axe working overtime.

Mind you, Darius didn't invent appraisal – Adam probably did that when he first inspected Eve and found things much to his liking. All we can say is, the process is as old as history itself. As further proof of the pudding, consider what the Roman poet Horace (65–8 BC) had to say in the way of laudatory appraisal about two of his contemporaries:

> For a just man and one with a firm grasp of his intentions, neither the heated passions of his fellow-citizens ordaining something awful, nor the face of a tyrant before his very eyes, will shake him in his firm-based mind.
>
> If the world should break and fall upon him, its ruins would strike him unafraid.

Praise indeed! Now, since it's always a good idea to kick off from square one, let's get the dictionary down from the loft and see what it says about 'appraisal':

APPRAISAL, *noun*: An appraising; official valuation.
APPRAISE, *tr. verb*: 1   To make an official valuation of; set a price or value on, especially by authority of law or agreement of interested parties. 2   To estimate the amount, quality or worth of; judge.

Right, so now you know . . . By the way, it's worth noting that bit, *by authority of law or agreement of interested parties*. So far as appraisal by one's boss is concerned, it's taken centuries for the concept of so-called 'open' (i.e., mutually discussed and agreed) assessment to gain any form of credence. Clearly, Big Daddy Darius wasn't overly concerned with getting his governors to agree that demerits would cost them their heads; but while (in some quarters, at least) capital punishment does not appear on today's appraisal menu, the dire old habit of 'closed', unilateral assessment continues to be top of the pops with far too many employers. We'll be returning to this topic in some detail a bit later on; in the meantime, let's get back to breaking the ice with what I like to call a mini-selection of appraisal bygones.

Not surprisingly, governments have always been front-runners in the appraisal rat-race. Throughout the ages, politicians of all colours and creeds have been faithful adherents of the process as a handy means of currying favour or back-stabbing their opponents; and, of course, since time immemorial, the world's civil and armed services have taken a positive delight in utilizing performance-cum-personality assessment as a means of weeding and seeding their respective hierarchies. I reckon it's worth taking a swift gander at some relevant examples:

He is one of those orators of whom it was well said, 'Before they get up, they do not know what they are going to say;

when they are speaking, they do not know what they are saying; and when they sit down, they do not know what they have said'. (Winston S Churchill, speaking of Lord Charles Beresford during a speech in the House of Commons on 20 Dec 1912).

This young Clerical Assistant excels at everything except punctuality, courtesy, powers of written and verbal communication, ability to follow simple instructions – and the basic will to work. (An 'I'll-get-him-this-time' salvo fired by a civil servant boss, who, for decency's sake, shall remain anonymous. The hapless chappie was subsequently (and rightly) hauled over the coals by his chief for resorting to sarcasm within an annual report.)

I esteem his *person* alone as equal to *one* French 74, and the *Superb* and her Captain equal to two 74-gun ships. (Extract from Admiral Lord Nelson's despatch of 11 July 1803 to Hugh Elliot, British Minister to Naples, appraising the redoubtable Captain Richard Keats, commander of HMS *Superb*.)

This officer sets a low standard which he consistently fails to maintain. (The apocryphal classic known to all officers of the British armed services who've dabbled more than a toe in the appraisal pond.)

Y'know, one cannot really appreciate the historical backcloth to our subject without considering that quintessential driving force of the Industrial Revolution, the Victorian employer. Although Benjamin Disraeli took every opportunity to declaim his 'two nations' of the Rich and the Poor, we all know that things weren't quite so clear-cut as that. Squatting just beneath the very rich in the pile was the comparatively newborn but lustily prosperous middle-class, who, in its turn, ruled the roost over the lower-middle-class traders, small manufacturers and other lesser businessmen. Last and very much least (if, that is, we discount the hapless unemployed), came the vast army of working-class folk, damned to eternity in the eyes of their self-pronounced betters as godless, ignorant, ungrateful, disobedient and rebellious. The point is, one of the weapons used by those who were determined to preserve this Victorian *status quo* was – yes, you've guessed it – appraisal.

One swallow doesn't make a summer, but feast your eyes on the letter that follows, written by an Industrial Revolutionist boss to one of his employees:

Ernest Thring & Co.,   8th October, 1844
Importer & Shipping Agent,
14 Botolph Lane,
Eastcheap,
City of London.

Sir,
I find it my bounden duty to remind you of that which transpired at yr. interview of earlier this day. In writing thus, it is yr. employer's earnest & prayerful hope that his words will caution you to improve yr. presently dilatory & idle approach to yr. daily labours – and, by this means, seek to restore his faith in yr. ability to render him good and diligent service.

It is not for the first time during some eleven years in yr. Master's service that he has found it necessary to caution you on yr. overall attitude to yr. responsibilities – which, to say the least, are light in their extent and in full accord with yr. generous terms of service. Despite these several warnings, you have persisted in arriving late at the Office on numerous occasions, thereby absenting yourself from Daily Prayers and ensuring a disgracefully late commencement of yr. working day. In addition, you have ensured the disapprobation and discomfort of yr. working colleagues on many occasions during the past winter by yr. failure to contribute yr. rightful share of coal for the office stove – thereby subjecting them to an unjust and undeserved burden. You have also displayed a less than punctilious attitude to Mr Blackthorne, the Senior Clerk – particularly on those occasions when he has found it necessary to remind you of yr. shortcomings.

For all these several reasons, I now confirm that yr. Weekly Remuneration of 9s. 8d. is reduced by 2s. 8d. (to 7s. 0d.) as from this date – and that any further misdemeanour on yr. part, however slight, will result in yr. immediate dismissal from my employment.

Yrs, etc., etc.,

Ernest Thring

To George Elwin Thomas, Clerk,
Residing at 13 Gregory Place,
Bartholomew Close,
Smithfields.

It's to be hoped that the recalcitrant Thomas took this evident appraisal-cum-final warning very much to heart, for there's little doubt that, once branded with dismissal for his various sins, he would have found it extremely difficult to land another job. Incidentally, if we measure Ernest Thring Esq. against those unyielding standards of Victorian rectitude, there's equally little doubt that he was a pretty decent employer, for in those halcyon days disciplinary warnings were few and far between. The quick bullet was indeed the order of the firing day . . .

Apart from Darius the Great, goodness knows who first introduced formal staff appraisal as a regular feature of working life. Since I have no intention, however, of presenting you with an academic treatise, I reckon it matters little. But there are one or two historical milestones worthy of note, and, for my money, the glorious wartime saga of the War Office Selection Boards, or 'Wosbees', as they were called, merits definite pride of place. Now, lest you're wondering why I'm choosing to plonk my size elevens in the selection arena, think on't. Aye, that's it in a nutshell: selection is all about the appraisal of people – so let's get on with the tale.

Largely because the government marched backwards into what we somewhat euphemistically describe as World War II, the Army found itself suddenly and desperately short of officers (to say nothing of NCOs and squaddies), and had to do something about it, but fast. Doubtless much midnight oil was burned before the red-tabbed General Staff and its political masters came up with the answer, the ubiquitous WOSBs. These hastily formed bodies were in effect *ersatz* selection sausage machines, designed and administered by (a) Army officers, who were culled for their expertise from heavens knows where, (b) 'suitably experienced' civil servants from the War Office, and (c) bevies of lip-smacking psychologists. As I've already intimated, the somewhat daunting task of the WOSBs was to dig among the eventual thousands of candidates and come up with nicely intelligent, self-disciplined and moderately gung-ho chappies who, potentially at least, could lead their men into battle – and, perhaps, back out again.

Much of what went on behind the WOSB doors, particularly in the early days of the war, can only be described as assessment nonsense. In fact we should thank our lucky stars that many of the very characters that the process was intended to highlight possessed sufficient gumption to see through the oft-rank amateurism of the Boards – and perform accordingly. This practice of 'fixing' or 'fudging' the various exercises and interviews became almost a contest of wits between the selectors and the more with-it candidates. After all, one has only to consider the type of loaded interview questions which were regularly thrown at the latter to understand why they (and, of course, umpteen skates) came through with flying colours:

COLONEL BLIMP (*fixing the candidate with what he fondly believes is a gimlet-sharp gaze*): 'Now, er, tell me, my man, why do you think you are fit to receive the King's Commission?'

Whereupon the wily candidate launches into a carefully rehearsed, suitably modest but sufficiently impressive exposition of personal characteristics which he knows full well will be music to old Blimp's ears.

COLONEL BLIMP: 'Harumphh, splendid – now, my boy . . .'

Or, for example:

PSYCHOLOGIST: (*resisting the temptation to pose the question, 'And when did you last see your father?' Instead, he produces a thoroughly dismal, Tale of Two Cities-type picture of an abject-looking prisoner. The tattered creature is depicted pulling himself up to the bars of his diminutive cell window, and is plainly engaging in a desperate bid to catch a glimpse of the blue sky beyond . . .*) 'Please look at this picture. Tell me, what is the first thing that comes into your mind?'

Aha, thinks the candidate, the gloom-and-doom bit! This is where I must exhibit an oh-so-healthy, mature but nicely imaginative turn of mind. All right, me bucko, you've asked for it . . .

But – and this is where we return to our theme – for all their many failings, the War Office Selection Boards created an involuntary foundation stone for what in peacetime was to become the very gradual spread of formal appraisal to the civvy-street workplace. Numbers of ex-service employers remembered the WOSB philosophy and, although their early efforts reflected exactly similar (and often far worse) brands of assessment bumbledom, things did start to happen, though on a very small scale. In short, so far as business and industry in the good old UK was concerned, the 1950s saw the birth of a troublesome, wart-ridden management baby – but, all too clearly and like it or not, one that was basically healthy and definitely here to stay.

The second and more recent milestone in this potted history of appraisal also concerns the British armed forces, but, this time, it's a tale of a very different calibre. Throughout the last thirty-odd years, the succession of service chiefs charged with the protection of this country have striven by every means at their disposal to introduce an extremely high level of professionalism throughout the army, navy and air force; and, despite the oft scandalous efforts of their political masters, have achieved eminent success. One vital facet of this continuing determination to create armed forces second to none is, of course, the requirement that personnel of all ranks are trained and developed to the peak of their individual proficiency, and it doesn't require much imagination to understand that this can only be done if every man and woman is subjected to regular, in-depth and *valid* performance appraisal. It should therefore come as little surprise to learn that, of all the organizations in this sceptred isle (with the possible exception of the Civil Service, which, generally speaking, has been equally keen), the armed services have devoted most time and money to the question of research and development in appraisal.

'Huh, I'm not surprised – after all, when one's got a mountain of taxpayers' money to play with, one can do anything . . .'

If that is your view, well, I'm sorry, because I don't intend to get drawn into that type of discussion! The point is, we folk in business and industry can only benefit from this extensive, well-founded research; if, that is, we have the inclination and the energy to get off our corporate butts and do something about it.

All of which brings me to the point where it's only necessary to bid you hullo, and welcome. I hope we've broken the ice. All that now remains is to get the show well and truly on the road. Stick with me while I set out to convince you that there's a lot of practical value in them thar appraisal hills.

THERE'S MORE THAN ONE WAY OF KILLING THE CAT

Think in terms of staff appraisal and one's mind automatically conjures up a picture of the boss appraising the hell out of a bunch of subordinates. This is only natural, since appraisal by one's senior is plainly the time-honoured, almost sacrosanct method of going about it. In one respect, this is a mite unfortunate, for there are two other approaches which have been proved time and time again to be a jolly sight more accurate.

Eh, really? What could be more accurate than Big Daddy's considered appraisal of his minions, which, bearing in mind his vantage-point, will constitute an admirable distillate of all his regular observations over a particular period of time? After all said and done, who is better suited than the boss to note and inwardly digest Jack or Jill Junior's revealed strengths and weaknesses? Isn't it the gaffer who, for fear of dying an executive death, is required to manage his people, and, as an inevitable consequence, maintain a watching brief on their progress?

Well, firstly, the hard fact is that *appraisal by Jack or Jill's peers* will always result in a more accurate picture than that produced by their boss. I'm probably teaching you to suck eggs, but it must be said that it's our working colleagues who rub shoulders with our relative strengths and weaknesses. They're the folk who swiftly tumble our good and bad attributes, our abilities and foibles – far better and far more intimately than any boss. The big snag is, we're British – dammit! – and our beloved adherence to custom and practice could well ensure that peer appraisal is never much more than a management pipedream.

If peer appraisal is accurate, then the remaining approach, *appraisal by one's juniors*, is DEVASTATINGLY accurate, and probably for that single reason will never be allowed breathing space within the hallowed confines of any manager's baili-wick. Just imagine, if our jobs depended on the considered views of our subordinates, why, half of us would be out of work in no time flat. Those who bear the yokes – the lads and lassies who, whether they like it or not, are saddled with our multifarious weaknesses and idiosyncrasies – would very soon ensure that justice was done . . . So, once again, I'll clamber out on the proverbial limb and offer that, so far as our lifetimes are concerned, anything like general acceptance of appraisal by one's juniors is strictly for the birds.

Last but by no means least, let me bring one other method of appraisal in from the cold – to wit, the good old business of *self-appraisal*. Suffice it to say that you're going to find quite some mention of this useful process in the pages that follow.

All right, my friend, that's that, introduction-wise. I reckon it's time to take a slurp at your favourite tipple, cos you're surely going to need it.

2 Getting down to brass tacks

As we gathered from our dictionary definition, appraisal is concerned with evaluation. It follows, as the night the day, that *staff* appraisal is concerned with the assessment and evaluation of people's displayed attributes, abilities and whatnot at work. But, as I'm sure you'll appreciate, the business of appraisal is by no means confined to the jolly old work scene – in fact, it's part and parcel of our individual struggle for existence in this human herd. Being animals at heart, from the time of our birth to the fateful day when we turn our toes to the sky, we spend a great deal of time and energy 'weighing up the opposition', considering alternatives, or evaluating our position in the light of various circumstances – in short, we appraise for survival.

Given our constant practice at the game, one could be pardoned for thinking that the requirement to cap our involuntary and everlasting appraisal of people at work with the trappings of a formally imposed scheme would present little in the way of difficulty. But, pardoned or not, such thoughts would be terribly wide of the mark. Unfortunately for Doris and Bertie Lazybones, there is a whole heap of difference between the automatic and basic human trait to which I have referred and the deliberate design and implementation of a formal appraisal scheme within an organization.

But before we 'go formal', as it were, it behoves us to take a peep at what goes on in terms of informal appraisal at work. For example, I think you'll agree that any employment usually kicks off with some form of appraisal – traditionally confined, heaven help us, to the wildly subjective selection interview.

And when one thinks about it (and teacher says you should), this process of evaluation, however subjective, tends to continue throughout every facet of working life. We all indulge, and don't we just, in evaluating our superiors, our peers and our colleagues, and – horror of horrors! – everyone does it to us. Very few working days go by without some discussion and argument concerning the worth and capability *of* workers, supervisors and managers, *by* workers, supervisors and managers. With precious few exceptions, all this frenetic, informal chuntering is also highly subjective and, as a consequence, more often than not invalid. But the point is, it happens. All of which can be a sobering thought, especially when one remembers that it is from this process that most appointments, pay rises, promotions, and dismissals stem.

So, there's a form of backcloth to our topic. Perhaps it is the one that prompts responsible and forward-thinking organizations to do something about improving and formalizing the appraisal process – to strive for some more realistic method of performance evaluation. Which, dare I say it, is what this book is all about.

PAVING THE WAY

There is nothing to be gained and much to be lost by leaping willy-nilly into the implementation of a formal appraisal scheme, and it's no exaggeration to say heaven help any management or individual who thus blasts off from square one without some really hard thinking. I make no apology for ramming this point home with a vengeance. Despite umpteen evidential horror stories of things badly done, employers still persist in either introducing a poorly designed appraisal scheme, or making a complete hash of a good one, and then proceed to cry hysterically into their beer when things blow up in their damned silly faces. The golden rule must be, HANDLE LIKE EGGS – and you'd better believe it!

Ideally, the vital preliminary study should constitute a two-fold exercise:

First stage

- Come up with an answer to the $64,000 question: *what is the purpose of the intended scheme, and will it actually satisfy this requirement?*
- Determine whether those responsible for the project appreciate that the scheme may not bear anything like fruit until some two years' assessment/validation of the resulting appraisals has been completed. Or, to put it more bluntly, ensure that the worthies concerned accept that the 'wanted yesterday' (or flamin' tomorrow) rule cannot possibly apply.

Second stage

- Arrive at a logical decision on the process of evaluation to be employed, i.e, get the nuts and bolts of the scheme exactly right.
- Consult with the appraisers, who, after all, are the operators who will make or mar the scheme, however good it may appear on paper or in the minds of those who have dreamed it up.
- Arrange adequate training and, where necessary, in-depth tuition/guidance in attitude-changing for the appraisers.
- Ensure skilful preliminary and ongoing communication with the appraisees, who, after all, are the people who are going to bear the brunt of the scheme, good or bad. Choose to ignore this one and, I promise you, you're dead.
- Again, confirm *exactly* how the forthcoming appraisal data is to be used – counselling, identification of training needs, career development, promotion, award of salary increments, or what-have-you.

ALL RIGHT, SO WHAT ARE THE VARIOUS USES OF AN APPRAISAL SCHEME?

If a management's heart is in the right place, it will wish to use appraisals for the 24-carat purpose of improving personal performance – and good on them! However, there are other applications and the following wee table indicates what these are, and to what approximate extent each is used by organizations already implementing appraisals:

Appraisal as a means of selecting people for promotion or transfer	65%
Appraisal as a means of determining individual pay increases*	62%
Appraisal as a basis for counselling for job enrichment and motivation	60%
Appraisal as a means of identifying individual training needs	60%

*A word of caution. Despite the relatively heavy use of appraisals as a means of determining individual pay awards, there is a growing body of opinion that this is a misuse of the process. Certainly, as I hope to illustrate later in this book, the appraisal interview is no place for a haggle over money. I'd keep the entire question of pay well away from the appraisal scene.

All of which brings us to what I regard as the major crossroads in this decision-making process, namely, the well-nigh crucial business of selecting the *method* of appraisal which, taking every possible factor into account, is best suited to one's corporate needs. I've no doubt that you already bear the scars to prove that important decisions in management are rarely straightforward, and I'm afraid that, once again, you're about to come face to face with a definitely ticklish problem of choice.

But, first, let us stick like glue to the rules for coming up with sound decisions and review the alternatives.

A SUMMARY OF APPRAISAL TECHNIQUES

Overall or 'basic' assessment
This technique simply requires that appraisers compile written reports on their subordinates at prescribed intervals. These write-ups may be completely unstructured (in which case, the barn doors of subjectivity will be shoved open to their widest extent), or the appraiser may be prompted to stick to certain narrative lines by the provision of a checklist highlighting such traits of personality as dependability, initiative, loyalty and so on.

Guideline or 'triggered' assessment
The only real difference between guideline and overall assessment is that the technique aims to obtain more specific judgements by requiring the appraiser to make separate comment against given characteristics; which, of course, can range like the March winds from such items as job knowledge and application of knowledge to powers of leadership and appearance.

Grading or 'forced choice' assessment
The technique of grading seeks to reduce subjectivity further by not only presenting a list of personal characteristics, but defining the various levels of quality in respect of each item so listed. The appraiser is required to consider each characteristic and select which of the given definitions most closely describes the appraisee; for example:

Physical fitness
Excellent – Eminently fit, always able to maintain performance.
Satisfactory – Able to maintain adequate levels of work even when tired.
Fair – Tends to slow down when slightly tired.
Unacceptable – Tires easily; weak and physically frail.

Rating

This technique carries grading a stage further, in that it requires the appraiser to rate each characteristic on an alphabetical or numerical scale, with or without guideline 'triggers', for each level of quality and with or without supporting narrative comment.

Results-orientated assessment

This grand-sounding heading is merely jargon for management by objectives. In this variation, agreed aims and standards of performance are established in advance and the subsequent appraisal is conducted on the basis of actual results, rather than on this and that itemized personal quality of the appraisee – thereby, it is hoped, obtaining greater objectivity.

There, then, are the choices – so, *quo vadis?*

COMING TO A DECISION, TECHNIQUE-WISE

Of the five alternatives, I strongly recommend that you reject the first (overall or 'basic' assessment) out of hand. Though attractively simple, the technique is fraught with the dangers of rampant subjectivity and will do little but harm to your appraisal cause.

To save you looking back, that leaves us with:

(a) guidelines or 'triggered' assessment;
(b) grading or 'forced choice' assessment;
(c) rating;
(d) results-orientated assessment.

I suggest that we can now further and substantially narrow our field of choice by noting one thing; namely, that if the broad history of appraisal is anything to go by, alternatives (a), (b) and (c) represent developmental stages of what, for the purposes of our decision-making, we can regard as one technique. For ease of reference, I suggest that we term this single process, 'rating assessment'.

So far so good – but I'm afraid we have yet to cross the proverbial Rubicon. If you're with me thus far, we're left with deciding which of two manifestly disparate alternatives to adopt:

(a) rating assessment, OR
(b) results-orientated assessment (the management by objectives approach).

And it's at this point that your author-chappie is going to throw you to the wolves by stating:

'*I'm sorry, my friend, but the decision is all yours* . . .'

One has only to glance at the current appraisal scene to be faced with one inescapable fact: we have a divided camp. While there are many organizations, big and small, which have nailed their flag to the rating mast (with fair accuracy, one could term them the 'traditionalists'), there are just as many organizations (the 'innovators'?) who spurn the technique in favour of results-orientated assessment. It's my intention therefore to drag you screaming by the ears on a two-prong approach to our subject – the Churchillian idea being that, having thus given you the tools, you then can finish the job. Chapters 3 and 4 will deal with the rating approach, and Chapter 5 with results-orientated assessment. Who knows, once we've ploughed those stony fields, I may even succumb to a somewhat battered ego and tell you which technique I prefer. But, and here's the rub, the decision's still down to you – you're a manager, and that's what you're paid for . . .

In the meantime we have a few more basic topics to kick around, so let's get on with them.

Another big decision – who is going to be appraised?
When Big Daddy takes the decision to introduce formal appraisal, it'll often be couched along the lines, 'Right, then, Carruthers, set up a scheme. That'll knock the beggars for

six . . .' And poor old Carruthers is left holding the baby, wondering whether it's best to confine the thing to the managers (which'll probably trigger him into including or excluding supervisory grades, depending on whether he's a modern, with-it thinker or a mummified Industrial Revolutionist), or, on the other hand, whether the scheme should cover everyone from the floor-sweeper upwards. And, of course, he's got a point, for which aspect of cogitation there are some remarkably unhelpful tips:

- Of all the organizations implementing formal appraisal, only about one-third extend their schemes to cover all employees.
- The indications are that, of this one-third, the majority utilize their appraisals for the primary purpose of determining pay awards – against which, for what it's worth and as you'll have gathered, I've set my cap.
- If the intended purpose is to assess fitness for promotion, then, ergo, the scheme should be confined to potential promotees.
- If career development is the intention, then – oh, Solomon of Solomons! – the coverage of the scheme should be as wide as possible.

It's up to you. Just remember that vital, preliminary study.

The timing of appraisals
There's little doubt that a properly administered appraisal scheme requires a good deal of work and, of course, consumes a fair old chunk of that priceless commodity, time. There's equally little doubt that frequent appraisals are well-nigh valueless and totally counterproductive. Consequently, many organizations administer their schemes on an annual basis, with most of them ensuring that individual appraisals are actioned on appointment anniversary dates, thereby spreading the load.

However, I'd recommend that, if and when it comes to the

crunch, you pinch a leaf from the armed services manual, namely, that you adopt the annual rule, but with the additional requirement that a supplementary appraisal is completed on occasions of promotion or transfer – needless to add, to be carried out by the manager who 'loses' the character concerned.

Who should be privy to appraisal reports?

Let's grasp the nettle straight away. Should an appraisee be permitted to see the contents of each and every report raised on him or her, or, if you prefer jargon, should the system be 'open' or 'closed'?

Now this is where we plonk ourselves in a right old mess of pottage. You'll likely recall my reference to the extensive research into appraisal carried out by the UK armed and civil services. Well, the fact is, despite their ongoing studies, for years and years these four organizations have been unable to achieve across-the-board agreement on this fundamental issue.

To take but one case in point, the Royal Air Force has currently got its armour-plated knickers in a fair-sized twist. On the one hand, since annual reports on airmen and NCOs are centrally filed on computer, the provisions of the Data Protection Act 1984 have urged the powers-that-be to disclose every word to the individuals concerned – something they wouldn't have dreamed of doing before the law came along. On the other hand, the Air Secretary's branch at the Ministry of Defence (Air), which is responsible for the control and custody of *officers'* annual reports, is obviously still in the age of the quill pen (that's monstrously rude, Air Secretary, and I apologise – I meant microfilm), with the result that, since the Data Protection Act doesn't apply to these records, they remain as direly confidential as ever.

In truth, there is a charming mini-exception to this majestic example of overweening security, and that concerns the dreaded 'starred items' in the report form, which, since I'm no Peter Wright, I'll merely describe as items connected with certain aspects of social conduct. In the event – heaven help him! – that an officer is rated low on these, he is required to be informed in no uncertain terms of his waywardness, and therefore knows that he's scored 4 or under on a potentially career-busting scale. I'm reliably informed that 'debate continues' on the topic of whether or not the RAF should hop into the twentieth century and create a truly open scheme. (Hey, did I say *debate*? Crikey, t'was never like that in my day.)

I should add that the Army and Navy have different views, with each service affording varying degrees of 'openness' within their respective schemes. As for the Civil Service, the philosophy of the-more-closed-the-better is beginning to wane, in that appraisees can be *told* in detail about certain contents of their report and even have the bits read out to them, but, as I understand it, they're never, ever allowed to read the thing themselves.

Having said all that, let me turn the volume up to loud and clear: any appraisal scheme worth its salt should be OPEN. Reports should be read by the appraisee, signed by him or her as having been read, and used by both parties as a basis for healthy discussion. As we shall see later on, the appraisee should also be permitted to add any written comment in the space duly provided on the form for that purpose.

If you need any further convincing, reader, consider this:

Appraisals should be open because –
- Justice must be *seen* to be done.
- *Inter alia*, a manager must be required to justify every jot and tittle of what he has written *about* the appraisee *to* the appraisee.
- Closed schemes are the seed-beds of apprehension and conjecture by those who are subjected to them.

As for the general security of appraisal schemes, it goes without saying that all the reports and associated records should be held in the safe custody of a duly nominated, senior member of the outfit – stamped and treated as STAFF

CONFIDENTIAL. Furthermore, it should be made plain to any secretaries or clerks who are necessarily engaged in the administration of an appraisal scheme that it's a condition of their employment that they maintain the strictest confidentiality at all times. Any such breach of contract should quite rightly be regarded as gross misconduct on the part of the offender – it's that serious.

How are you faring? Before you have another slurp, spend a few minutes on Work Box Number 1. Oh, sorry, I didn't warn you! From now on, there'll be a wee task (sometimes more than one) at the end of each chapter – and you are on your honour to have a jolly good bash at completing them.

Work Box Number 1

Think appraisal (as if you'd be doing anything else) and, assuming that you've been tasked with formulating a *rating scheme* to cater for managers and supervisors, draw up a suitably comprehensive list of the items to be rated.

Don't concern yourself at this stage with *how* you would rate the items, because all that gubbins will come later. Once you've completed the task to your satisfaction, put it aside – we'll be having a tutorial in Work Box Number 2.

Work-tip. Beware of the danger of letting the whole thing become an exercise in semantics. Choose your items with care, ensuring that you steer clear of 'definition overlap' (e.g. the terms 'determination' and 'resolve' mean one and the same thing) and that they're relevant to your needs and readily identifiable by the average Jack or Jill Manager.

3 A detailed look at appraisal rating systems

Get any band of managers together and task them with deciding what their proposed rating scheme is to measure, and, quick as a flash, they'll come up with two eminently sensible items, *quality of work* and *quantity of work*. Give them a few more minutes of brainstorming and it's more than likely that they'll start screaming for a flip-chart:

- Quality of work.
- Quantity of work.
- Job knowledge.
- Powers of communication.
- Timekeeping.
- Attendance.

At this point there's likely to be a few 'ums' and 'ahs', but never fear – within a few seconds, they'll take a belly-flop dive into the murky waters of *'personal qualities'*. The duty flip-chart scribe will shift into overtime mode and the fun'll really start; for example:

- Reliability.
- Initiative.
- Co-operation.
- Loyalty to the company.
- Loyalty to one's subordinates.
- Enthusiasm.
- Judgement.
- Conduct.

- Ability to withstand stress.
- Sense of humour.
- Integrity.
- Sense of fairness.
- Self-confidence.
- Appearance and bearing.
- Determination.
- Foresight.
- Alertness.
- Poise.
- Creativity.
- Powers of leadership.
- Physical fitness.
- Tact.

Having got thus far, they'll likely run out of paper – and ideas.

You'll see from the above that our mythical band of managers have trodden the traditional path in formulating their list of qualities to be measured, i.e., they've attached great importance to the appraisal of A. N. Other as a *personality*. This is hardly surprising, because there are few, if any, of us who'd be happy to work over, alongside or under an android. Sheer common sense dictates that we managers do all in our power by way of expert selection, inspiring leadership (and, yes, sound appraisal) to ensure that our people 'fit in', personality-wise.

Which is all highly laudable. The trouble is, while one stands a very good chance of being able to quantify and thus rate such items as job performance, job knowledge, punctuality, attendance, etc., we find ourselves in a very different ball-park when it comes to the rating of so-called personal qualities. You may agree that there are two main difficulties:

- *Playing the quality word-game.* When formulating a list of personal qualities (PQs) to be measured, as mentioned in Work Box Number 1, it's very easy to let the whole thing degenerate into an exercise in semantics. We'll be dealing

with this aspect in Chapter 4, when we tackle the business
of designing *your* rating-type appraisal form.
● *Yes, the knotty old problem of subjectivity.* Let me put it this
way. My conception of young Murgatroyd's integrity, to
name but one PQ, is unlikely to accord with your
considered assessment, while colleague Jim, who, like us,
is also saddled with the frailty of arrant subjectivity in such
matters, will probably express a quite different view. All
of which must pose the question, who the hell is right?

Thus far in this book, I've tended to use such terms as
'measuring', 'rating', 'assessing' with somewhat gay
abandon, and I reckon the time has come when we should get
to grips with this important aspect of the appraisal process.
Let's do exactly that.

RATING SCALES IN GENERAL

Assessment rating scales or yardsticks weren't just introduced
to impress the boss, or confuse the innocent. Their purposes in
life are to ensure *as far as is possible* that:

(a) the ogre of subjectivity is minimized. The idea is that by
requiring job-holders to be rated on given scales, appraisers
are prompted to *think through* their associated narrative
comments, and *vice versa*. In a nutshell, ratings must justify
narrative, and narrative must justify ratings;
(b) the operators of the scheme are provided with a common
basis for comparing appraisees' assessments 'across the
board'. The use of rating scales will not rid the scheme of
subjectivity, but given that appraisers are adequately
trained, it will be reduced. Anyway, how d'you compare
narrative comments one with another – and come up with
anything like a near-objective result?

One can, of course, employ the simplest of rating methods;
for example:

- Does the employee co-operate with
  his/her colleagues?   Yes/No
- Does he display enthusiasm in his
  work?   Yes/No

I'd better mention that if you're looking for an appraisal with
'Yes/No' ratings, it won't be worth your trouble proceeding
further with this y'ere book – which'll be a crying shame if you
paid good money for it.

GRAPHIC RATING SCALES

It's safe to say that most appraisal schemes employ graphic
rating scales of one sort or another. At their simplest, each
quality to be measured is accompanied by either a range of
letters or numbers, and the appraiser is required to rate the
individual by circling the appropriate letter or number, thus:

	High *Low*
Reliability	A B C D E F
OR	
	High *Low*
Reliability	6 5 4 3 2 1

Before we take a look at variations of the above, there are three
points to bear in mind:

(a) Think in terms of using an EVEN-NUMBERED scale,
    thus making it impossible for appraisers to plonk their mark
    on the highly attractive, middle-for-diddle letter or
    number. Given such an opportunity, far too many will take
    the soft option and go for 'average'.
(b) Refrain from making the scale too extensive – or, for that
    matter, too short. The six-point scale, shown above, is ideal
    for most practical purposes; and, for more specialist appli-
    cations, the eight-pointer is about top-whack.
(c) Note also that numerical scales are used more often than
    their alphabetical counterparts. Certainly, numerical scales

make it much easier to construct profiles or calculate averages (of which more anon).

Apropos (b), above, a few years ago, a national retailing chain with an all-too-familiar name in the High Street proudly announced (as is its inveterate corporate wont) its brand new supervisory appraisal scheme; and, largely by devious means, I managed to get hold of the much vaunted, minute scrap of paper which purported to be its appraisal form. It bore two qualities, 'Performance' and 'Personality', and against each was the scale 'A, B, C, D'. However, I was quietly informed by a certain regional manager of the company that, so far as 'his' supervisors were concerned, there were certainly no 'D-types', and he had therefore instructed his branch managers to carry out appraisals based on the three-point scale 'A, B, C'. To cap everything, the two spaces for supporting narrative comment measured approximately 1 cm × 2 cm, each. So much for the company's oft-heard cry that it's super-efficient in all things, especially staff development.

Sorry about that! Let's get back to the question of improved graphic scales. One way in which the appraiser can be helped to make a more objective judgement is to cap the scale with more informative 'triggers', thus:

Exc.	V. Good	Above average	Below average	Fair	Poor
6	5	4	3	2	1

There is virtually no limit to this development of triggers; as depicted in the following part-example:

ACCEPTANCE OF RESPONSIBILITIES	A consistently outstanding and impressive leader	Always in the lead when the occasion demands
	6	5

Before we leave graphic scales, it's worth noting that a few of the beggars who design them are not above practising a smidgin' of artfulness. For example, by providing very detailed triggers which are not set down in ascending/descending order, together with letters or numbers which are apparently selected at random, it's possible to obscure the measurement process, and thus make it harder for appraisers, say, to manipulate scores in favour of blue-eyed boys or girls.

RANKING SYSTEMS

Ranking systems are not in widespread use as a process of formal appraisal, probably because the initial paperwork is not confined in the traditional manner to 'one report per individual' – far from it! The appraiser is required to rank a group of employees of similar status in descending order of assessment against each prescribed quality, for example:

QUANTITY OF WORK	*QUALITY OF WORK*
1 Andrews	1 Stewart–Smith
2 Stewart–Smith	2 Andrews
3 Metcalfe	3 Blake
4 Smith, W. G.	4 Metcalfe
5 Blake	5 Smith, W. G.
6 Downley	6 Downley

Ranking systems are relatively simple to operate but, unless the appraiser is happy to go prematurely grey, are only suitable for the assessment of small groups.

CHECKLIST RATING SCALES

Checklist scales merely require the appraiser to tick whichever phrase (from a selection provided for each quality) most closely describes the appraisee. Figure 1 is offered as a tongue-in-cheek example of a checklist scale – and that just about says it all.

	5	4	3	2	1
LEADERSHIP ABILITY	He can stand on my neck whenever he likes, gorgeous brute	Always manages to lead horses to drink	Knows how to spell 'leadership', anyway	Doesn't know how to spell it	Calls his wife 'Ma'am' when she allows him to speak to her
PERCEPTUAL ABILITY	Once drew the winner of the Grand National	Can tell in a flash when his desk is on fire	Has been known to tell the difference between chalk and cheese	Has crystal-clear awareness of his inability to solve any problem	Can always tell if a door is shut by the way he bruises his nose on it
MANUAL DEXTERITY	He can undress any woman in ten seconds, flat	Is inclined to use the office junior as a paperweight	Can always undo those cling film wrapped sandwiches	Can never undo cling film wrapped sandwiches	Was born with ten thumbs
ORAL ABILITY	Suffers from a malignant form of verbal diarrhoea	Always talks in his sleep – and expects replies	Inclined to lecture empty rooms	Has been known to utter the odd word or two	Grunts when prodded

Figure 1   A not-recommended example of a checklist rating scale

So, there it is – our mini-catalogue of rating scales. What we've got to do now is gird our loins and consider a fairly warty aspect of the art of 'scoring' in appraisals.

THE NITTY-GRITTY OF SCORING AND WEIGHTING

Imagine that the following is a section of boss George's appraisal of Billy Bloggs:

	High					*Low*
Quality of work	6	5	4	③	2	1
Quantity of work	6	5	④	3	2	1
Job knowledge	6	5	4	③	2	1
Safety habits	6	5	4	③	2	1
Attendance	6	⑤	4	3	2	1
Punctuality	6	5	④	3	2	1

So far as scoring his appraisal is concerned, George may elect to:

- Do nothing further, i.e. remain content with the picture or profile of Billy provided by the *raw scores* (the numbers he has circled) and draw his conclusions accordingly.
- Add up the raw scores to give Billy a total rating of 22, which he may then compare with the total ratings of other employees in similar categories/grades.
- In cases (admittedly rare) where several appraisers do their stuff on Billy, use the composite ratings to calculate an average or median score for the guy.

So far so good. However, it could be the case that when George, or whoever, designed the appraisal scheme, he thought fit to attach more importance to 'quality of work', 'attendance' and 'punctuality' than the other items on the list. In other words, it was decided to *weight* the higher level

numerical values relating to these three qualities, in which case
the appraisal form might well take the following form:

	High				*Low*	
Quality of work	8	7	6	③	2	1
Quantity of work	6	5	④	3	2	1
Job knowledge	6	5	4	③	2	1
Safety habits	6	5	4	③	2	1
Attendance	8	⑦	6	3	2	1
Punctuality	8	7	⑥	3	2	1

Plainly, weighting comes into its own when the appraisal
scheme either requires raw scores to be added up for direct
comparison with other employees' scores, or the 'averaging'
process is to be applied to several reports on Billy.

All of which brings us to the gloom and doom chunk . . .

APPRAISAL PITFALLS AND WEAKNESSES

No process concerned with *homo sapiens* is without its snags
and, by golly, there's no doubt that staff appraisal has its share!
I strongly recommend that you pay very good attention to the
Black Museum that follows, for each of the catalogued pitfalls
and weaknesses is a potential appraisal-killer.

Playing the 'rating game'

Let's face it, most managers dislike completing appraisals.
One salient reason for this antipathy is that many of them feel
that appraisal is not only an unpleasant chore, but also
something of an insult to their intelligence. They feel that they
already know 'their people' and, in essence, that any required
process of formal assessment is an unnecessary burden. Some
also feel that an imposed appraisal scheme constitutes a
deliberate challenge to their ability to judge the individuals
they're required to rate – which, of course, is quite correct. A
further and powerful disincentive is that managers are
required to 'dig deeper' when completing appraisals than they

would ever otherwise think of doing, and this takes time and effort.

As if all that were not enough, not a few managers entertain serious doubts about the validity and practical value of the scoring and/or weighting processes, etc., which have been foisted on them. They often feel that the whole thing has been cooked up by some non-revenue-earning leech in the Ivory Tower merely to justify his or her existence.

For these several reasons, it can often be the case that conscripted appraisers tend to treat the whole process as a game or contest, to be completed as swiftly as possible without true regard for thoroughness of approach or equity. Plainly, it only requires one manager to adopt this stance and, quick as a flash, his attitudes will become public knowledge throughout the workforce, and the scheme will be wrecked in the eyes of appraisers and appraisees alike.

The solution can only be sound training and attitude-changing.

The peril of varying standards

Brief any employees about the introduction of an appraisal scheme and it's a pound to a penny that they'll come up with the blockbuster doubt, 'How do we know that we'll all get the same treatment from our respective gaffers? Manager A's ratings are bound to be different to Manager B's, and that'll kick the whole thing into touch . . .' Without adequate training of appraisers, the very serious problem of varying standards *will* raise its head – so you've been warned.

Central tendency

The error of central tendency or 'middle-for-diddle' is the oft-natural tendency by appraisers to 'play safe' and rate all appraisees as average, or near-average; and, as you'll appreciate, there's no more effective way to castrate an otherwise effective scheme. Again, the one and only prophylactic is effective training.

Leniency

The over-generous or cowardly manager will tend to be lenient with his or her ratings, and that says it all. Remember, appraisal demands healthy discussion (yes, we're going to deal with that topic later on), and the latter type of appraiser will do anything to avoid an eyeball-to-eyeball disagreement.

Effective training is the answer.

Halo

Halo? No, we're not up with the angels on cloud nine. Halo is the very human tendency of appraisers to allow one quality to overshadow others, or to make all the rated qualities conform with some form of hazy general impression. Hence, as an example of the former weakness, an appraiser who is nuts on golf may thoughtlessly rate a subordinate who happens to be a fellow-golfer as the bee's knees in several other, totally unrelated qualities.

Effective training is needed.

Systematic errors

A systematic or constant error is an overweening tendency by some appraisers to overvalue or undervalue appraisees on a given quality or characteristic. Hence, one such offender may attach little importance to, say, 'personal initiative' and constantly award a low rating to those individuals who rightly deserve a much higher assessment.

Effective training, once more.

Total errors

These are an appraiser's degrees of variation above and below the ratings which, given the chance, other appraisers would award the self-same employee. In other words, total error is the offence committed by an appraiser whose approach, ratings-wise, is completely out of kilter with the norm.

And, yes, yet again, effective training is the ONLY answer.

On to Work Box Number 2, please!

Work Box Number 2

You'll need your 'list of qualities to be appraised' from Work Box Number 1 for this little task, so dig it out, please.

What I'd like you to do is quite simple and straight-forward, merely:

(a) Re-examine the list and ensure to the best of your ability that your chosen qualities really are as mutually self-exclusive as is possible.
(b) Without looking back over the chapter, devise suitable rating scales to accompany your list of qualities.

And don't dare to peep at the following tutorial until you've finished.

Tutorial to Work Box Numbers 1 and 2
Obviously I have no means of knowing what qualities you have listed, but I can offer a few tips on how best to approach this essential preliminary to setting up any appraisal scheme:

● At the risk of boring you to tears, the overall aim must be to make the selected qualities mutually self-exclusive – so, in a sense, one is really into pure semantics at this early stage. Outright synonyms in the appraisal context are definitely *verboten*.

Integrity	>	Honesty
Judgement	>	Discernment
Application	>	Diligence
Dependability	>	Reliability
etc.		

● Research indicates that the following items are those

---

most used by organizations already implementing formal staff appraisal:

Concerning the job	*Concerning the individual*
Quality of work	Reliability
Quantity of work	Initiative
Job knowledge	Co-operation
Attendance	Adaptability
Punctuality	Judgement
	Enthusiasm
	Leadership
	Application
	Conduct
	Intelligence

Do not be inclined to regard the above list as Holy Writ, but, rather, as some of us would regard, say, the Top Ten in the world of pop music.

Keep your list of choices to hand. You'll have a further opportunity to compare them with mine when we start designing your appraisal form in the next chapter.

So far as devising a rating scale for your qualities is concerned, I hope you remembered that the numerical graphic rating scale is the most widely used, and that suitably devised triggers are a great help to the poor old appraiser. Also, you should have noted the importance of making it an even-numbered scale (no middle-for-diddle choice for the safety-minded opportunist) and that it should not be too short or too extensive, for example:

6 5 4 3 2 1
or
8 7 6 5 4 3 2 1

T'would be nice if all the Work Boxes turn out to be as simple as Numbers 1 and 2, wouldn't it? Oh, boy, have I got news for you ... !

4 Designing your rating assessment form

I don't think it's a bad idea to kick off this chapter by introducing you to some of the prime exhibits in what I choose to call my Appraisal Form Chamber of Horrors. So, assuming that you can stand the sight of blood, I suggest we get cracking.

D'you recall my reference to the so-called appraisal form introduced by that nationwide chain of retailers? Okay, here it is, shrouded in anonymity, but otherwise presented in all its dubious glory (Figure 2).

Quite apart from the sheer banality of the attempt at appraisal depicted in Figure 2, there's an unseen sting in the tail. I'm told that the regional manager concerned used to carry out grand walk-around visits to his branches every six months or so; when, sticking rigidly to the wretched tradition, he'd pause here and there to burble 'Good day – how are you?' to every sixth or seventh member of staff. How the hell he managed to acquire personal knowledge of the poor old supervisor-appraisees is, to say the least, a good question yet, would you believe, he was the guy who decided whether or not each of the poor critters had earned a merit pay award! And, remember, this was the gaffer who'd decreed that none of his supervisors were to be rated as 'D' for performance or 'personality'. Yep, it seems that some mothers do 'ave 'em!

Our next exhibit really takes the cake, so cast your tired old peepers over Figure 3. This ghastly piece of invention was the *tour de force* of a personnel officer who, lacking qualifications and experience, tried to impress all and sundry with his expertise in appraisal. Sad to relate, an unwise boss sanctioned

```
┌─────────────────────────────────────────────────────┐
│                  STAFF APPRAISAL                      │
│                                                       │
│  Name _____  Branch No _____    │
│  Grade _____ Dept _____      │
│  Appraised by _____ Date _____       │
│                                                       │
│  PERFORMANCE     _____      │
│  A  B  C  D      Comment:                             │
│  PERSONALITY     _____      │
│  A  B  C  D      Comment:                             │
│                  _____      │
│  - - - - - - - - - - - - - - - - - - - - - - - - -    │
│  Confirmed by Area Director _____ Date _____    │
│  Action _____     │
└─────────────────────────────────────────────────────┘
```

*Figure 2   An appraisal form that effectively discounts
the old adage, 'Small is beautiful'*

its introduction, with the immediate result that the entire
management team rose in revolt. Bye, bye, personnel
officer . . . Once you've had a good look at the thing, see if
your conclusions agree with mine.

Here they are, listed in no special order:

(a) In addition to the fact that the nine-point scale really
stretches things a bit far for the non-specialist appraiser, the
damned thing dangles the middle-for-diddle carrot
squarely in front of their eyes. How would you like the task
of deciding whether Blenkinsop merits, say, a '3' or a '4' on
such a rating scale?

(b) *Gestures, facial expressions?* If an appraisee is addicted to
making continual V-signs at everyone, or is afflicted with a
grievous facial tic, how is one expected to rate the hapless
so-and-so – with a '1' or a '9'? Anyway, should such
extraordinary items appear on an appraisal form? By all
that's holy, they shouldn't!

Name _____Department _____
Appraised by _____ Date of review _____

MANNER AND APPEARANCE	Low	High
Gestures		1 2 3 4 5 6 7 8 9
Facial expressions		1 2 3 4 5 6 7 8 9
Speech		1 2 3 4 5 6 7 8 9
Poise		1 2 3 4 5 6 7 8 9
Personal hygiene		1 2 3 4 5 6 7 8 9
Courtesy		1 2 3 4 5 6 7 8 9
Height		1 2 3 4 5 6 7 8 9
Weight		1 2 3 4 5 6 7 8 9
Stamina		1 2 3 4 5 6 7 8 9

SOCIABILITY
Effectiveness of teamwork	1 2 3 4 5 6 7 8 9
Involvement in social activities	1 2 3 4 5 6 7 8 9
Involvement in local affairs	1 2 3 4 5 6 7 8 9
Friendly attitude	1 2 3 4 5 6 7 8 9

EMOTIONAL STABILITY
Inclined to bear grudges	1 2 3 4 5 6 7 8 9
Quick temper	1 2 3 4 5 6 7 8 9
Defensive reaction to failure	1 2 3 4 5 6 7 8 9
Difficult adolescent history	1 2 3 4 5 6 7 8 9
Lonely, poorly balanced life	1 2 3 4 5 6 7 8 9

MATURITY
Interest in extra-mural pursuits	1 2 3 4 5 6 7 8 9
Independence in decisions	1 2 3 4 5 6 7 8 9
Sense of responsibility	1 2 3 4 5 6 7 8 9
Economic drive	1 2 3 4 5 6 7 8 9
Logical career objectives	1 2 3 4 5 6 7 8 9

SUMMARY	BELOW		ABOVE
RATING	AVERAGE	AVERAGE	AVERAGE

Appraiser's signature _____ Post _____

Figure 3   An appraisal-monster clearly concocted by an idiot

(c) How d'you feel about *poise*? I wonder if your conception of this quality is the same as mine – that the item will tend to lead the appraiser into the minefields of *pure* subjectivity and varying standards. If the quality has to be used, it cries out for some form of explanatory trigger, does it not?

(d) Crikey, *personal hygiene*! While *standards of dress* or just plain *personal neatness* may be in order, I pity the appraiser who is required to rate (and presumably discuss) a subordinate's standards of personal hygiene. To quote but one example, the hardy perennial menace of the employee with rampant BO is something to be tackled 'as and when', certainly not shelved (ugh!) for the next appraisal session. Mind you, if one is appraising nurses or folk of that ilk, then the question of personal hygiene assumes a somewhat different hue. It's possible that our thoughts may differ on this item, and if they do, who on earth is right?

(e) How many bosses would be fully justified in appraising their subordinates' *height and weight*? If these items are, indeed, of importance, should they not have been investigated at the selection stage? If Little Willie shows signs of developing into a Billy Bunter *and his obesity is affecting his job*, is this not also a case of 'action as and when'?

(f) Passing quickly on, what about the method of scoring the items in general under the heading 'Sociability'? Again, if the appraisee is notably lacking in these minus qualities, how does one rate him – high or low? T'is not explained, is it?

(g) As for *difficult adolescent history* and *lonely, poorly balanced life* – well, I ask you! Methinks the anonymous designer of this form suffered in both respects. Make no mistake, reader, these are two outstanding examples of appraisal quackery.

(h) I pride myself on having middlin' to fair powers of comprehension, but I must admit to being somewhat stumped over the item *economic drive*. If you're a better man than I am, Gunga Din, you'll doubtless have an explanation, but do me a favour and keep it to yourself, will you .

(i) Now we come to the real beaut, the requirement

PERFORMANCE	Low				High	
Quality of work	1	2	3	4	5	6
Quantity of work	1	2	3	4	5	6
Willingness to work overtime	1	2	3	4	5	6
Attendance	1	2	3	4	5	6
PERSONALITY	Low				High	
Pleasant outgoing						
personality	1	2	3	4	5	6
Dictatorial/discursive	1	2	3	4	5	6
tendencies	1	2	3	4	5	6
Inclined to introversion	1	2	3	4	5	6
Prone to question authority	1	2	3	4	5	6
Loyalty						
PERSONAL CHARACTERISTICS	Low				High	
Undesirable characteristics						
Behaviour under stress	1	2	3	4	5	
	1	2	3	4	5	
Potential	1	2	3	4	5	

Figure 4   Some more wart-bearing appraisal snippets

(presumably) to plonk one's appraising mark on BELOW AVERAGE, AVERAGE or ABOVE AVERAGE. How does one set about arriving at this decision, bearing in mind the scoring difficulties mentioned in (b) and (f), above? The short answer is, close one's eyes and pin the tail on the donkey – it'll be as accurate a means as any other approach.

Having thoroughly panned that one, let's pass on to the next exhibit. Figure 4 depicts a selection of appraisal snippets which I've culled from this and that company appraisal form over the years. See how they grab you.

Once again, I'd like you to compare your thoughts on the items in Figure 4 with mine:

(a) in the first snippet, there's been no attempt to weight the higher level ratings relating to any of the listed qualities. If, therefore, it was decided to tot up the raw scores in this section (for the purpose of gaining an average, or not), it would be possible, for example, that a thoroughly unproductive tyke who scored well on *willingness to work overtime* and *attendance* could gain an unrealistic overall total. Weighting should always be considered if it is decided that raw scores are to be totted up.

(b) in the second snippet, we have super evidence of selected qualities which are not mutually self-exclusive, particularly in the case of *pleasant outgoing personality* (oh, joy!) and *inclined to introversion* – with *prone to question authority* and *loyalty* coming a close second. The snippet also provides yet another shining example of that nasty old evil, ambiguity, where the scoring requirements are concerned. Does the appraiser rate low or high for 'good' or 'bad'?

(c) in our third snippet, your eagle eye should have flown to that masterpiece *undesirable characteristics*. Ho, hum, the mind boggles. Presumably the appraiser would have been under instructions to check if any of his subordinates were going blind . . . But, do be warned, while this snippet is blatantly peurile, it is very easy to fall into the trap of introducing 'cover-all', blanket-type items into one's list of qualities and traits to be measured.

(d) next, the fourth snippet. *Potential*? Potential for what, pray: making trouble, promotion to MD-designate, giving blood, or what? As I hope to show later on, items to be measured must be stated in clear and concise terms – otherwise your cherished appraisal scheme will be plunging hell-bent for disaster.

(e) last, but certainly not least, I hope you noticed that the anonymous authors of the last two snippets have employed a five-point, middle-for-diddle scale. To be scrupulously fair, quite a few managers favour the use of odd-numbered scales, arguing that, since many employees *are* average, appraisers should be given the opportunity of rating them as such. By now it should be plain that I do not take this view. As stated earlier, I believe that the absence of a middle position on the chosen scale constitutes, at the very least, a trigger for some objectively inclined thought – with, just perhaps, the consequence that the ratings will reflect a bit more accuracy.

It's my hope, if nothing else, that our brief romp through the Chamber of Horrors will have put you in a cautious mood, because we've now got to chomp on the meat in this chapter's sandwich, i.e. the design of *your* appraisal form. Hey, hang on . . . On due reflection, I think I should qualify that big-headed intention. The real aim is to invite you to work with me on producing some practical and fairly detailed appraisal paper-work, with the end result that you'll then be better equipped to produce your own, hand-tailored stuff. Yes, I think that sounds more like it, so let's get on.

SETTING THE PARAMETERS

First of all, I propose that we indulge in good management practice and cook up some basic requirements. For better or worse, then, here they are.

- We'll imagine that 'our' appraisal scheme is to cater for all grades of junior managers, including supervisors, throughout the company.
- Thankfully, our directors are wholly committed to:
  - (a) the introduction of an ongoing programme of individual career development;
  - (b) effective training as a vital prerequisite of corporate and individual success;
  - (c) a policy of promotion from within whenever realistically possible;
  - (d) fostering and maintaining individual job satisfaction and good employee relations.

  In the light of this encouraging climate, we decide that the appraisal scheme is to provide a basis for:
  - (a) bilateral assessment and discussion of an individual's performance during the period under review; and, arising from this, the mutual identification and agreement of future performance objectives;
  - (b) identification of individual training needs;
  - (c) highlighting and assessment of promotion potential;
  - (d) contributing to individual job satisfaction as a result of the discursive/counselling measures entailed in (a) and (b), above.
- We'll also imagine that we opt for an annual appraisal system, with the rider that, unless a routine appraisal has been completed within three months of the event, an appraising manager must complete a further report whenever any junior manager or supervisor is promoted or transferred away from his or her charge.

Doubtless you'll have noted the significance of that reference to *'bilateral assessment . . . of an individual's performance . . .'*. However, just in case the point happened to escape your attention, this means that our junior managers and supervisors will be invited to carry out an exercise in *self-appraisal* before the 'main event'. Thus both parties at the big session will be armed with their individually prepared appraisals, and these two documents will form the prime basis of the ensuing discussion. This means, of course, that we are about to design TWO appraisal forms, and, just for the hell of it, I suggest that we tackle the self-appraisal first.

Before we spring into action, I'd just like to add that we're going to spend some time on this twofold task, and, because I wish you to be fully armed, our design will include all the nitty-gritty details, even down to a suggested layout for the front cover page of each form. If, therefore, you're only interested in the end-products and really couldn't care less about the mechanics of producing them, then *stop reading this chapter and go straight to the back of the book*, where you'll find the two completed forms reproduced for your lazy-bones attention in the appendices.

DESIGNING A SELF-APPRAISAL FORM

The cover page

Setting out the cover page is a straightforward task, provided that one remembers there are three basic requirements to be fulfilled:

(a) The *security aspect*. If many organizations (particularly the smaller, less formalized outfits) do have an inherent security weakness, it is almost certainly in the area of personnel management, in general, and in the handling of 'personnel paperwork', in particular. You may recall my passing reference in Chapter 2 to the paramount need for completed appraisal documents to be classified STAFF CONFIDEN-TIAL, and it may well be the first time you've come across this particular classification. You may even be wondering why on earth it's necessary to employ anything other than the customary, single word, CONFIDENTIAL. Well, the answer to that one is, everyone above a given level in the average company (if there is such a thing) is usually privy to material marked 'confidential', *but personnel documents are a completely different kettle of fish, and should be treated as such.* When it is common knowledge among employees that 'their' often intensely personal paperwork is open to scrutiny by every Tom, Dick and Harriet, respect for management is airborne and heading for the window. So, whether you deem it nit-picking or not, a STAFF CONFIDENTIAL grading is the order of the appraisal day.

(b) The *administrative aspect*. Plainly, it helps things to tick over smoothly if the employee who has completed the form is easily identifiable – and, remember, someone has to do the filing.

(c) The *guidance/motivational aspect*. The cover page should bear an encouraging message on the use of the self-appraisal after completion, and, unless instructions are included within the body of the form (which will be the case with ours), some guidance on how best to complete the form.

So, with these three requirements in mind, perhaps you'd care to look at Figure 5.

Having 'set' the cover page of our self-appraisal form (by the way, note the use of the none-emotive word 'review' in Figure 5), I think it's high time that I emphasized one important point. While you may be inclined if the mood gets you to slavishly copy any of the layouts in this book, my prime intention is that you should utilize them as triggers for your own creative abilities. After all, while it's fine and dandy to follow the ground rules, there's really nothing to beat hand-tailored documentation, especially in appraisal – is there, me hearty? So, 'ave a bit of pride, do!

The skills to be self-appraised
I propose that the main body of our self-appraisal form should focus the employee's attention on three main areas of assessment.

STAFF CONFIDENTIAL

Name _____
Job Title _____
Dept _____

Review Period _____

**PLUNKETTS LTD
SELF-APPRAISAL REVIEW**

NOTES FOR YOUR GUIDANCE

This self-appraisal review is intended to achieve a number of objectives:

(a) to provide a framework for the forthcoming discussion with your manager;
(b) to enable you to assess your overall performance during the period under review;
(c) to enable you to highlight any additional training which you may feel you require in order to perform your job more effectively;
(d) to help you and your manager to reach agreement on any personal aims which you may seek to achieve during the coming year.

In the event that you have any queries regarding the completion of this review, please do not hesitate to seek the advice of your manager.

Figure 5   The cover page of a rating assessment self-appraisal form

- People-management skills.
- Resource-management skills.
- Organizing skills.
- Communication skills.

Furthermore, in order that the form meets our criteria, the employee should not only be required to assess his/her competence in respect of each item listed (remember, by way of numerical graphic scales supported by narrative comment), but should also examine the question of any associated training that may be considered necessary.

Have a brief think about how you would set about fulfilling these requirements, and then examine Figure 6 with care.

A SELF-ASSESSMENT OF YOUR 'PEOPLE-MANAGEMENT SKILLS'

Please consider your current performance in terms of the abilities listed below. Utilizing the scales provided, you are asked to assess your existing level of competence in each ability by circling the appropriate number. Kindly justify each assessment by commenting in the space provided.

1 The ability to manage your team by earning their respect, organizing them decisively and inspiring them to greater effort

I am confident that I organise and inspire my team to give of their best	>>>>>> 6 5 4 3 2 1 <<<<<<	I know that I am inefficient in the use of my team; I engender low morale

Comment _____

_____

_____

Can you think of any training that would improve your competence in this area? Brief comment, please.

_____

_____

2 Competence in appraising the actual and potential performance of your team members, discussing with each member his/her personal strengths and weaknesses, and counselling with tact and good judgement

Figure 6　The body of the self-appraisal form

I am confident in   >>>>>>   I lack the ability
my complete   to carry out
ability to carry   effective apprai-
out effective   6 5 4 3 2 1   sal and coun-
appraisal and   selling
counselling   <<<<<<

Comment _____
_____
_____

Can you think of any training that would improve your competence in this area? Brief comment, please.

_____
_____

**3 The ability to handle all disciplinary and griev-
ance matters with the necessary degree of
fairness, firmness and patience**

I am confident   >>>>>>   I am unable to
that I handle   handle these
these matters   6 5 4 3 2 1   matters in the
exactly in the   manner descri-
manner descri-   <<<<<<   bed
bed

Comment _____
_____
_____

Can you think of any training that would improve your competence in this area? Brief comment, please.

_____
_____

Figure 6 The body of the self-appraisal form (contd)

4   The ability to actively develop the work skills and knowledge of all members of your team by indentifying individual training needs, implementing or arranging the required training, and maintaining adequate training records

I am confident that I carry out these functions with regular and eminent success   >>>>>>

6 5 4 3 2 1

<<<<<<

I am unable to carry out these functions with any degree of success

Comment_____

_____

_____

Can you think of any training that would improve your competence in this area? Brief comment, please.

_____

_____

5   A full understanding of the positive motivation of people at work and the ability to create and maintain the right conditions for it

Yes, I am a consistently effective and excellent motivator   >>>>>>

6 5 4 3 2 1

<<<<<<

I do not possess this understanding or this ability

Comment_____

_____

_____

Figure 6   The body of the self-appraisal form (contd)

Can you think of any training that would improve your competence in this area? Brief comment, please.

_____

_____

A SELF-ASSESSMENT OF YOUR 'RESOURCE-MANAGEMENT' SKILLS

6 The ability to make full and economic use of all machinery, equipment and materials within your control

| I am confident that I am a fully proficient manager of the resources within my control | >>>>>>

 6 5 4 3 2 1

 <<<<<< | I do not possess the ability to effectively manage the resources within my control |

Comment _____

_____

_____

Can you think of any training that would improve your competence in this area? Brief comment, please.

_____

_____

7 The ability to effectively discharge all your financial and accounting responsibilities, including (where this is applicable) financial estimating, costing, budgeting, reporting and controlling; working within estimates; the maintenance of relevant accounting records and the handling of cash

Figure 6   The body of the self-appraisal form (contd)

I am confident that I fully and effectively discharge all such personal responsibilities	>>>>>> 6 5 4 3 2 1 <<<<<<	I fail to effectively discharge such personal responsibilities

Comment _____

_____

_____

Can you think of any training that would improve your competence in this area? Brief comment, please.

_____

_____

A SELF-ASSESSMENT OF YOUR ORGANIZING SKILLS

8　The ability to organize, in general

I consider that I am a consistently excellent organizer	>>>>>> 6 5 4 3 2 1 <<<<<<	I consider that I am a muddled thinker who works without system

Comment _____

_____

_____

Can you think of any training that would improve your organizing ability (e.g. training in forecasting, planning and allocating work; stock planning, purchasing and control; defining objectives and setting

Figure 6　The body of the self-appraisal form (contd)

standards; project management; personal time management; work analysis; organization and methods; interpretation of plans and data, etc.)? Brief comment, please.

_____

_____

A SELF-ASSESSMENT OF YOUR COMMUNICATION SKILLS

9 The ability to communicate verbally with your subordinates in such a manner that understanding and informative feedback is assured

I am confident   >>>>>>   I am ineffective
that I put my
points across   6 5 4 3 2 1
convincingly
and concisely   <<<<<<

Comment_____

_____

_____

10   Written communication

I am confident   >>>>>>   My written work
that my written   is clumsy and
work is always   6 5 4 3 2 1   obscure
cogent,   clear
and well set out   <<<<<<

Comment_____

_____

_____

Figure 6   The body of the self-appraisal form (contd)

Can you think of any training that would improve your competence in verbal or written communication? Brief comment, please.

_____

_____

Thank you for completing this self-assessment. If you wish to make any further comment which you consider is relevant to your forthcoming performance review, please do so. _____

_____

_____

_____

_____

_____

_____

Signed _____Date _____

Figure 6   The body of the self-appraisal form (contd)

Needless to say, we will deal with the manager's use of the self-appraisal form in a later chapter. What we now have to do is tackle the main gubbins – the appraisal form, proper.

DESIGNING AN APPRAISAL FORM

The cover page
Once again, designing the cover page is quite straightforward. Obviously we need to be consistent, so I've used the cover page of the self-appraisal as our model. However, if you look at Figure 7, my suggested layout, you'll see that the appraiser's attention is drawn to something called 'Notes for Guidance – Completion of the Staff Appraisal Report! No sweat, cobber! Once we've completed the form itself, we'll go on to consider this important adjunct to the process.

The main body of the appraisal report
As regards this form (which, let's face it, is the crux of the entire process), there are a number of important things to note. I therefore suggest that, having examined Figure 8, you keep one eye glued to it while reading what follows – it'll certainly help if you can manage such an ocular contortion . . .

- Unlike the self-appraisal form, the items to be rated and duly commented upon are divided into two sections, headed 'Performance' and 'Personal Qualities'.
- Since the intention is that the employee will produce his or her completed self-appraisal at the time of the appraisal discussion (*and not before*), certain items in the form, indicated by an asterisk, relate to those in the self-appraisal (Figure 6). The appraiser is thus reminded that the employee's self-rating (plus comment) should be compared with his or her own rating (plus any relevant comment) in each case. While the subsequent discussion should not be confined to an examination of these items alone (remember, our scheme is entirely 'open'), the asterisks should help the appraiser to pick out those of his ratings which will figure in this direct comparison.

STAFF CONFIDENTIAL

Name _____
Job Title _____
Dept _____
Appraised by _____

Review Period _____

**PLUNKETTS LTD
STAFF APPRAISAL REPORT**

IMPORTANT Before completing this report, please refer to the pamphlet, 'Notes for Guidance – Completion of the Staff Appraisal Report'. If you are not in possession of this guide, please obtain a copy from the Personnel Manager.

Figure 7   The cover page of a rating assessment appraisal report

- Some rating scales have been duly weighted.
- Provision has been made for the totting-up of raw scores and 'averaging', if required.
- Where relevant, the appraiser is required to express an opinion regarding the suitability of the appraisee for promotion.
- The appraisee is required to make recommendations for training, where relevant.
- The form caters for comment by the appraiser's senior, or, at the very least, for certification by that worthy to the effect that the report has been duly considered and agreed.

PART A   PERFORMANCE

Overall aspects of performance

1   Job knowledge

| Has exceptionally thorough knowledge of all aspects of the job and can apply this knowledge | >>>>>>
 765321
 <<<<<< | Is very seriously deficient in all aspects of job knowledge |

Comment_____

_____

2   Proficiency in current post

| Is outstandingly proficient in all aspects of the job | >>>>>>
 765321
 <<<<<< | Incapable of producing acceptable standards of work |

Comment_____

_____

Figure 8   The body of a rating assessment appraisal report

3 Resourcefulness as a manager/supervisor

Is exceptionally resourceful and constructive in his/her approach to the job	>>>>>> 7 6 5 3 2 1 <<<<<<	Is notably lacking in any originality and thought

Comment _____

_____

_____

4* Ability to organize (see Figure 6, Items 1/8)

Is an outstanding organizer and planner	>>>>>> 7 6 5 3 2 1 <<<<<<	Lacks organizing ability; works without any apparent system

Comment _____

_____

_____

5* Ability as a leader (see Figure 6, Item 1)

Is a consistently outstanding and inspiring leader	>>>>>> 7 6 5 3 2 1 <<<<<<	Avoids the responsibilities of leadership at every opportunity

Comment _____

_____

_____

Figure 8   The body of a rating assessment appraisal report (contd)

6   Attendance

Is absent only with very good reason	>>>>>> 6 5 4 3 2 1 <<<<<<	Is often absent without good reason

Comment _____

_____

_____

7   Punctuality

Is an exceptional timekeeper	>>>>>> 6 5 4 3 2 1 <<<<<<	Is frequently late for work without good reason

Comment _____

_____

_____

8   Willingness to work overtime

Always works excess hours willingly	>>>>>> 6 5 4 3 2 1 <<<<<<	Dislikes and shirks overtime

Comment _____

_____

_____

Figure 8   The body of a rating assessment appraisal report (contd)

Composite rating

$$\_+\_+\_+\_+\_+\_+\_+\_=(\_)$$

Specific aspects of performance

9   Competence in delegation

Is exceptionally proficient as a delegator	>>>>>> 6 5 4 3 2 1 <<<<<<	Is a consistently poor delegator

Comment _____

_____

_____

10*   Competence in performance appraisal and counselling of subordinates (see Figure 6, Item 2)

Is exceptionally proficient as an appraiser and counsellor	>>>>>> 6 5 4 3 2 1 <<<<<<	Is incapable of conducting any form of appraisal or counselling

Comment _____

_____

_____

Figure 8   The body of a rating assessment appraisal report (contd)

11*   Competence in handling disciplinary and grievance matters (see Figure 6, Item 3)

| Is exceptionally competent in the handling of all matters of a disciplinary or grievance nature | >>>>>> 654321 <<<<<< | Is incapable of handling any matters of a disciplinary or grievance nature |

Comment _____

_____

_____

12*   Non-specialist competence in the identification of subordinates' training needs, implementation or procurement of the training required and the maintenance of training records (see Figure 6, Item 4)

| An exceptionally capable non-specialist trainer | >>>>>> 654321 <<<<<< | Is incapable of handling any aspect of his subordinates' training |

Comment _____

_____

_____

Figure 8   The body of a rating assessment appraisal report (contd)

**13*   Competence in the art of positively
motivating subordinates** (see Figure 6, Item 5)

Outstanding in   >>>>>>   Is incapable of
every respect as   understanding
a motivator of   6 5 4 3 2 1   or practising the
employees   art of
                        <<<<<<   motivation

Comment _____
_____
_____

**14*   Competence in the full and cost-effective
utilization of all machinery, equipment and
materials within his/her control** (see Figure 6,
Item 6)

An exceptional   >>>>>>   Is an incapable
manager of all   manager of all
such resources   6 5 4 3 2 1   such resources

                        <<<<<<

Comment _____
_____
_____

**15*   Competence in relevant financial and/or
accounting duties** (see Figure 6, Item 7)

Is outstandingly   >>>>>>   Lacks
competent in   competence in
every respect   6 5 4 3 2 1   all such duties

                        <<<<<<

*Figure 8   The body of a rating assessment appraisal
report (contd)*

Comment _____

_____

_____

Composite rating

__+__+__+__+__+__+__= (__)

Communication skills

16*   Oral expression (see Figure 6, Item 9)

| Excellent: speaks convincingly and concisely | >>>>>>
 6 5 4 3 2 1
 <<<<<< | Is an ineffective speaker |

Comment _____

_____

_____

17*   Written expression (see Figure 6, Item 10)

| Excellent: always cogent, clear and well presented | >>>>>>
 6 5 4 3 2 1
 <<<<<< | Is ineffective; written work is very clumsy and obscure |

Comment _____

_____

_____

Composite rating

__+__ = (__)

Figure 8   The body of a rating assessment appraisal report (contd)

PART B PERSONAL QUALITIES

18   Sense of duty

Outstanding in every respect: is consistently eager and enthusiastic	>>>>>> 6 5 4 3 2 1 <<<<<<	Invariably places self before duty

Comment _____

_____

_____

19   Judgement

Excellent: his/ her proposals and decisions are invariably sound	>>>>>> 6 5 4 3 2 1 <<<<<<	Very poor: is prone to many and varied errors of judgement

Comment _____

_____

_____

20   Reliability under stress

Excellent: he/ she is consistently unflustered and competent	>>>>>> 6 5 4 3 2 1 <<<<<<	Very unreliable, even under normal circumstances

Comment _____

_____

_____

*Figure 8   The body of a rating assessment appraisal
report (contd)*

21   Co-operation

Excellent: he/ she is consistently sensitive to the feelings/ problems of others and earns great respect	>>>>>> 6 5 4 3 2 1 <<<<<<	Totally lacking in co-operation and fails to earn the respect of others

Comment_____

_____

_____

22   Appearance and bearing

Is exceptionally smart at all times – a credit to his employer	>>>>>> 6 5 4 3 2 1 <<<<<<	Slovenly in every respect

Comment_____

_____

_____

Composite rating

__+__+__+__+__ = (__)

*Figure 8   The body of a rating assessment appraisal
report (contd)*

PART C TRAINING RECOMMENDATIONS

_____
_____
_____
_____

PART D RECOMMENDATION FOR PROMOTION

(a) If not recommended for promotion, state reasons
_____
_____

(b) Recommendation for normal promotion:

Recommended ( )   Strongly recommended ( )

Comment _____
_____
_____

(c) Recommendation for special/accelerated promotion

Comment _____
_____
_____
_____

*Figure 8   The body of a rating assessment appraisal
report (contd)*

PART E FOR COMPLETION BY APPRAISEE

I have discussed my Self-Appraisal Review and this report with my manager and I have the following comments to make _____

_____

_____

_____

_____

_____

_____

Signature of Appraiser _____ Date _____

Signature of Appraisee _____ Date _____

PART F COUNTERSIGNING MANAGER'S REPORT

_____

_____

_____

_____

_____

_____

_____

Signed _____ Date _____

Figure 8   The body of a rating assessment appraisal report (contd)

Unless I'm way off beam, reader, your reaction to the appraisal form depicted in Figure 8 (and, for that matter, the self-appraisal in Figure 6) is most unlikely to be one of pure acceptance. The alternatives are many and various, and here are just a few:

'Far too complicated – how many hours d'you think there are in a day? I've got better things to do than even contemplate putting in a scheme of that nature . . .'

'I don't agree with this, or that – or the other . . .'

'Quite honestly, I just want something that my managers can bash off over a quick cuppa.'

'Rubbish . . .'

Apart from reminding you that the two examples are primarily intended to serve as triggers for thought, I've little choice but to plunge straight into the full broadside mode – and stress as I've never stressed before that, while a well designed and administered appraisal scheme can be a most effective management tool, a bad 'un can be positively lethal in its effects on morale. So, while you may not feel inclined to go along with the samples I've shoved in front of you, for goodness sake be careful when knocking together your own little masterpieces!

Let's get on.

THE VITAL 'NOTES FOR GUIDANCE'

Figure 9 depicts a set of 'notes for guidance' for your consideration – once again presented with the aim of whetting your thinking appetite. See what you think of 'em.

STAFF CONFIDENTIAL

PLUNKETTS LTD

NOTES FOR GUIDANCE
COMPLETION OF THE STAFF APPRAISAL REPORT

Introduction

Used in conjunction with the Self-Appraisal Review, the Staff Appraisal Report is a key aid to good management within the company. The completed report is designed to present information in a useful form for the purposes of:

- Promoting meaningful dialogue between the manager and employee at the appraisal discussion.
- Assisting management to identify training needs and make decisions on the career development of the employees concerned.
- Assessing fitness for promotion or transfer.
- Implementing suitable action in cases of inefficiency, etc.

In order that these aims can be achieved, please ensure that you are thoroughly familiar with these notes before participating in the staff appraisal process.

Figure 9   'Notes for Guidance' to accompany the appraisal form depicted in Figure 8

Completing the report

The Staff Appraisal Report requires you to 'rate' or assess the employee in respect of listed abilities/ personal qualities which cover most aspects of his/ her work and contribute to job performance:

PART A PERFORMANCE

Overall aspects of performance

Job knowledge.
Proficiency in current post.
Resourcefulness as a manager/supervisor.
Ability to organize.
Ability as a leader.
Attendance.
Puctuality.
Willingness to work overtime.

Specific aspects of performance

Competence in delegation.
Competence in performance appraisal and counselling of delegates.
Competence in handling disciplinary and grievance matters.
Non-specialist competence in the identification of subordinates' training needs, implementation or procurement of the training required and the maintenance of training records.
Competence in the art of positively motivating subordinates.
Competence in the full and cost-effective utilization of all machinery, equipment and materials within his/her control.
Competence in relevant financial and/or accounting duties.

Figure 9 'Notes for Guidance' to accompany the appraisal form depicted in Figure 8 (contd)

Communication skills

Oral expression
Written expression

PART B   PERSONAL QUALITIES

Sense of duty.
Judgement.
Reliability under stress.
Co-operation
Appearance and bearing.

You are required to rate the appraisee in respect of each item by circling the appropriate score on the six-point scale and making relevant narrative comment in the space provided. *In taking care to evaluate each of the abilities/personal qualities separately, you should ensure that your narrative comment justifies the allotted score in each case, and vice versa.*

When determining scores, beware of any tendency to rate the employee as 'average' on a number of items instead of being more critical in your judgement. Beware also of rating him/her as 'excellent' or 'poor' on a number of items merely because your overall impression is one of excellence or inadequacy, i.e., take particular care to identify the employee's undoubted strengths *and* weaknesses, and rate accordingly.

Composite ratings When you have completed the ratings in each section, calculate the composite rating by recording and totalling your elected scores in the space provided.

Figure 9   *'Notes for Guidance' to accompany the appraisal form depicted in Figure 8 (contd)*

Part C – Training Recommendations Complete this section *after* you have discussed the question of further training with the employee and taken into account his/her views (as expressed within the Self-Appraisal Review *or* during discussion).

Part D – Recommendation for Promotion If you are not recommending the employee for promotion, clause (a) *must* be completed.

Part E – For Completion by Appraisee Once the appraisal discussion has been completed, the employee should be invited to record his/her comments on the outcome of the process. He/she should be asked *either* to make full and frank comment (in particular, regarding any points or issues on which it has not been possible to achieve mutual agreement), *or* enter the words 'No comment', as he/she deems appropriate. It is stressed that no attempt should be made to inhibit or otherwise influence the employee at this stage of the appraisal.

You should then sign and date the report and ask the employee to do the same.

Part F – Countersigning Manager's Report The completed Staff Appraisal Report and the employee's Self-Appraisal Review should be forwarded under confidential cover to your countersigning manager without delay.

Figure 9 'Notes for Guidance' to accompany the appraisal form depicted in Figure 8 (contd)

Would you believe it, that's about all for this chapter – except, of course, that you've got Work Box Number 3 looming up on the horizon . . .

Work Box Number 3

You'll need bags of hard thought for this task, but, once tackled, it does have the advantage (says he, with infinite optimism) of providing you with some useful ammunition for your real-life appraisal efforts. All you have to do is compose suitably graded triggers *for each score* on six-point scales for the abilities/personal qualities listed below. To make things easier, we'll kick off with an example of what I mean.

JOB KNOWLEDGE

6	5	4
Has an exceptionally thorough knowledge of all aspects of the job	Possesses very comprehensive job knowledge	Possesses a more than satisfactory level of job knowledge

3	2	1
Possesses a fairly satisfactory level of job	Some deficiencies in job knowledge	Is unacceptably deficient in job knowledge

Okay, now it's your turn. Compose six graded triggers in respect of each of the following items:

(a) Acceptance of responsibility.
(b) Effectiveness in control.
(c) Reliability.
(d) Self-confidence.

Remember to be a good Scout, and restrain your urge to, er, cheat.

Tutorial to Work Box Number 3

I wish we could get together on this one, because I'm sure we'd have a lively discussion; but we can't, so here are some suggested examples for comparison with your sterling efforts.

ACCEPTANCE OF RESPONSIBILITY

6	5	4
Is consistently outstanding in the acceptance of responsibilities	Invariably accepts responsibility when the occasion demands	More than usually willing to accept responsibility

3	2	1
Willing to accept responsibility	Only inclined to accept responsibility when told	Deliberately avoids accepting responsibility

EFFECTIVENESS IN CONTROL

6	5	4
Outstanding in every respect as a controller of staff	Extremely effective as a controller of staff	Very effective in control

3	2	1
Competent in control	Not always competent in control	Incapable of exercising control

RELIABILITY

6	5	4
Outstandingly reliable. His word is his bond	Extremely reliable in almost all circumstances	More than usually reliable in all normal circumstances

3	2	1
Usually reliable in all normal circumstances	Tends to be unreliable; has to be supervised	Unreliable and irresponsible

SELF-CONFIDENCE

6	5	4
Displays consistently outstanding and completely justifiable self-confidence at all times	Displays consistently high degree of self-confidence based accurately on knowledge and experience	Displays a more than satisfactory level of self-confidence in all normal circumstances

3	2	1
Normally self-confident	Sometimes over-/under-confident	Habitually overconfident; seldom admits to being in the wrong – OR habitually underconfident; weak and indecisive

Now, it may well be that you're one of those gifted souls who can sling beautifully apt words together in a trice; in which case, you'll have raced through this exercise like a dose of salts. If, however, you're like me and the wretched words don't come easily, well, take comfort in the fact that you're not alone – and get in some solid practice, especially with triggers!

5 A detailed look at results-orientated systems

At first glance, the advantages of results-orientated appraisal are obvious and persuasive:

(a) because the process is wholly concerned with reviewing a job-holder's actual performance against mutually agreed standards and targets, it is a jolly sight more objective;
(b) when properly administered, it steers the appraiser away from simple criticism of this and that aspect, requiring, instead, that he *helps* the job-holder to improve his performance;
(c) the appraisee takes an active part in examining and evaluating his own performance, and is thus better equipped to tackle the task of improvement.

However, like everything in management, there are a number of potential snags. By far the biggest problem is the sobering fact that, to be effective, *management by objectives* (we'll abandon that 'orrible term, results-orientated appraisal) is intensely time consuming to implement, and will never enjoy success unless everyone in the executive hierarchy from Big Daddy downwards is wholly committed to the cause. As if that were not enough, there are other complications that can seriously beset any MBO programme:

(a) The mechanics of the process demand that its practitioners operate extensive and costly control-cum-audit systems.
(b) The business of agreeing targets is fraught with risk. For example, a manager may propose objectives which are

quite wrong, and, knowingly or unknowingly, an appraisee may accept them.

(c) Given the unlikely event that all members of management are committed to the principles of MBO, it will be necessary to undertake considerable and expensive training of appraisers in its implementation.

In order to illustrate what MBO entails, let's summarize the process. First, having obtained the necessary commitment of all and sundry, you must conduct an in-depth study of each subordinate's job – *to the extent that standards of performance, or OBJECTIVES, are mutually agreed for each and every specific duty or responsibility*. Thus, for a manager or supervisor, the study will be required to include agreed objectives in respect of the individual's:

- General duties and responsibilities in relation to the common functions of management, i.e. planning, organizing, staffing, supervising, directing, controlling, coordinating and innovating.
- Specific duties and responsibilities as listed in his or her up-to-date and, again, mutually agreed job description, which, of course, every thinking boss will have ensured is present and ready for inspection.

Once all the objectives have been mutually agreed, the subsequent appraisal takes the form of a *discursive counselling session* (kindly note the emphasis, and that Chapter 7 deals with appraisal counselling in some detail). The session will concentrate on how things have worked out during the period under review, and, in the light of the outcome, exactly how the individual is going to tackle the future in terms of agreed intentions and objectives. Not infrequently, before the get-together, the employee will be required to complete a self-appraisal on his or her performance, and the comparison of this with the appraiser's assessments will form a basis for the discussion.

Now let's add some meat to the bones.

THE ALL-IMPORTANT JOB DESCRIPTION

The hard fact is that, contrary to my ill-warranted sarcasm just now, far too many managers contrive to get by without ensuring that their subordinates are armed with job descriptions. Playing out the executive role with their tunnel vision riveted on what they mistakenly regard as the bottom line, such uninformed folk often describe the production and maintenance of job descriptions as a pointless, money-wasting exercise, fit only for bumph-generating management-idlers. Well, suffice it to say that if you want to implement MBO, you've no choice but to accept that these documents are an absolutely crucial prerequisite for success.

I don't expect you need reminding, but just in case the old memory is not what it was, here is a skeleton make-up of a typical job description:

1 *Identification* The job title, grade and, if applicable, department concerned.
2 *Reporting to* Expressed by job title, not name.
3 *Purpose of the job* A statement of the objectives of the job.
4 *Duties* A statement of the main duties of the job.
5 *Responsibilities* A statement setting out the job-holder's main responsibilities for personnel, equipment, materials, money, etc.
6 *Relationships* A statement of the relationships involved in the job, both inside and outside the organization, expressed in terms of job titles.

SETTING OBJECTIVES

You'll probably have noticed that, in bashing out the foregoing stuff, I've made pretty hefty use of the words 'mutually agreed', and, believe me, this was quite intentional. The pig's orphan of a manager who believes he can practise MBO by unilaterally imposing objectives on his subordinates would do well to consider my favourite management truism:

> *In business, as elsewhere,*
> *HUBRIS is the unforgiveable sin of*
> *acting cocky when things are going*
> *well. As the Greeks tiresomely told us,*
> *HUBRIS is followed inexorably and*
> *inevitably by NEMESIS . . .*

The demanding task of developing and setting objectives *cannot* be other than a responsibility shared between job-holder and manager. If Joe Soap is to understand and appreciate the purpose of MBO, if he's to have any abiding interest in the aims of the organization of which he's an essential part, he must be encouraged to exercise *his* innate judgement and job knowledge in evolving personal objectives. Having completed what is essentially an exercise in motivation, the manager has then to leaven, where necessary, his subordinate's proposals with a measure of realism and practicality, and, once mutual agreement has been achieved, highlight the yardsticks against which *both parties* will measure the job-holder's subsequent performance.

One has only to read between the lines of the last paragraph to realize that, so far as Jack or Jill Manager is concerned, the setting-up and implementation of MBO is no sinecure, and you'd better believe that it can separate the executive wheat from the chaff in no time flat.

'All right, ALL RIGHT, I get the message – so less of the flaming exhortations, if you please. You blithely refer to the business of 'setting objectives', but this can be damned difficult at the best of times. What about some practical tips, for a change?'

My friend, I hear yo' call. The process of actually putting one's finger on targets, let alone quantifying them, can be the cause of a heap-big headache, indeed. So here is a form of route-planner, intended to plonk you on the right road to setting a few typical objectives:

| FACTOR | SOME AREAS TO EXAMINE WITH A VIEW TO SETTING OBJECTIVES |

Management
- *Responsibilities in general*   Which personal responsibilities dissatisfy the job-holder?
- *Delegation*   Has the job-holder cleared his own job of all the routine 'doing' tasks? How effective is his/her delivery of orders and instructions? To what extent does he/she conduct an audit of delegated tasks? What are the results, in terms of success or failure, of his/her delegation?
- *Problem-solving and decision-making*   To what extent is the job-holder directive/consultative in his/her approach? What relative strengths/weaknesses are highlighted by a review of his/her results in this area?
- *Leadership*   To what extent does he/she successfully cater for (a) the individual needs, (b) the group needs, and (c) the task needs of his/her team? To what extent does his/her management style reflect an authoritative, paternalistic, consultative/participative approach? To what extent is he/she inclined to be 'people-centred' or 'things-centred' in management?
- *Sociability*   To what extent does his/her style tend to be distant/aloof or open/friendly?

Specific work responsibilities
- Acceptance of responsibility?
- Extent of professional/technical knowledge in the area concerned?
- Application of professional/technical knowledge in the area concerned?
- Application of professional/technical skills in the area concerned?

GETTING TO GRIPS WITH THE PAPERWORK

If appraisal via MBO is to stand any chance of success, it follows as the night the day that the associated forms must be up to scratch, reflecting, probably above all, the participative approach to the technique. It may be a bit late in the day to remind you that countless, otherwise genuinely altruistic schemes in all walks of life have foundered on the rocks of ill-designed, curt, jargon-ridden paperwork – and appraisal is no exception. That said, and sticking rigidly to my customary rule of thumb when providing illustrations of what I mean, the forms that follow are not intended to be slavishly copied, but are offered as triggers for constructive thought.

DESIGNING AN 'MBO-TYPE' SELF-APPRAISAL FORM

The cover page
If you care to glance at Figure 10, you'll see that the cover page illustrated is almost a carbon copy of our earlier example in Figure 5, which it jolly well should be, since the parameters involved are virtually identical, i.e.:

(a) the document must be classified STAFF CONFIDEN-TIAL;
(b) for administrative ease, the employee is identified;
(c) the thing must encourage the self-appraisee to get stuck in and do his considered bit.

The contents of the self-appraisal form
I suggest that the first aim of the form should be to require the job-holder to 'validate' his or her current job description, that is to say:

(a) having itemized the main responsibilities listed on the JD, the employee should then indicate whether or not these still apply by entering the percentage of time spent on each one;

STAFF CONFIDENTIAL

Name _____
Job Title _____
Dept   _____
Review Period _____

PLUNKETTS LTD
SELF-APPRAISAL REVIEW

NOTES FOR YOUR GUIDANCE

This self-appraisal review is intended to achieve a number of objectives:

(a) to provide a framework for the forthcoming discussion with your manager;
(b) to enable you to assess your overall performance during the period under review;
(c) to enable you to highlight any additional training which you may feel you require in order to perform your job more effectively;
(d) to help you and your manager identify and mutually agree your personal goals during the coming year.

In the event that you have any queries regarding the completion of this review, please do not hesitate to seek the advice of your manager.

Figure 10   The cover page of an 'MBO-type' self-appraisal form

(b) the opportunity for the employee to record newly acquired responsibilities should be provided. These responsibilities do not appear on the current JD, either because it simply hasn't been amended, or because, true to fashion, the things have just 'crept in' without being officially delegated by management.

Then, remembering that the entire caboodle must be performance-orientated, the form should provide ample opportunity for the job-holder to:

(a) assess his or her performance during the period under review;
(b) frankly identify any snags or hang-ups which hindered progress;
(c) suggest ways and means of improving future performance;
(d) make at stab at setting future goals.

Take a long, hard look at Figure 11. Does this sample form fulfil all the above objectives, or, as is almost certainly the case, is there room for improvement? Well, don't just sit there like a stuffed dummy – get cracking, friend!

PART 1   A REVIEW OF YOUR MAIN JOB RESPONSIBILITIES

Kindly itemize your main job responsibilities, exactly as listed in your current Job Description, and provide an indication of the percentage of working time spent on each one.

Responsibility	% of time

It may well be that you have assumed primary responsibilities that are *not* listed on your Job Description. If so, please itemize these, and provide an indication of the percentage of working time spent on each one.

Figure 11   The body of an 'MBO-type' self-appraisal form

Responsibility	% of time

PART 2   A REVIEW OF YOUR YEAR'S WORK

What aspect of your year's work do you consider you have done best, or with greatest satisfaction? In your view, how could these strengths be exploited to benefit you and the company?

_____
_____
_____
_____
_____

What do you consider you have done least well, or with least satisfaction? In your view, how could these relative weaknesses be overcome?

_____
_____
_____
_____
_____
_____

Figure 11   The body of an 'MBO-type' self-appraisal form (contd)

It may well have been the case that you were hindered in some aspect(s) of your work by organizational or other problems. If this was so, please describe the impediments, and suggest how they could be overcome in the future.

_____

_____

_____

_____

_____

_____

_____

PART 3   IMPROVING YOUR CAPABILITIES

Please consider all the aspects of your job. In your view, what additional training and/or work experience do you require in order to improve your capabilities?

_____

_____

_____

_____

After due consideration, you may well feel that certain organizational/procedural changes (additional to any mentioned by you in Part 2, above), acquisitions of equipment, etc., would enhance your capabilities. If so, please describe what you think is necessary.

_____

_____

_____

Figure 11   The body of an 'MBO-type' self-appraisal form (contd)

PART 4   PLANNING FOR YOUR FUTURE

Please refer to the responsibilities listed by you in
Part 1 and, in particular, to those which occupied the
bulk of your working time. Bearing in mind that a
prime purpose of the forthcoming appraisal discussion is to set your mutually agreed objectives for
next year, what do *you* think should be your key
goals for the period?

_____
_____
_____
_____
_____
_____
_____
_____
_____

Looking ahead, what do you intend (or hope) to be
doing in three to five years' time? How do you see
your career developing?

_____
_____
_____
_____
_____
_____
_____

*Figure 11   The body of an 'MBO-type' self-appraisal
form (contd)*

So much for the self-appraisal form. Now let's move on to the gaffer's version.

DESIGNING AN 'MBO-TYPE' APPRAISAL FORM

Ramming home the obvious, the two-fold purpose of the 'MBO-type' appraisal form is to provide:

(a) a basis for friendly, frank and completely open discussion between the manager and his subordinate;
(b) a yardstick which, used in conjunction with the self-appraisal, will facilitate an in-depth, discursive review of the job-holder's past performance and mutual agreement of his or her goals for the future.

Once you have examined the sample form depicted in Figure 12, we'll take a gander at the accompanying 'Notes for Guidance'.

STAFF CONFIDENTIAL

Name _____
Job Title _____
Dept _____
Appraised by _____

Review Period _____

**PLUNKETTS LTD
STAFF APPRAISAL REPORT**

IMPORTANT Before completing this report, please refer to the pamphlet, 'Notes for Guidance – Completion of the Staff Appraisal Report'. If you are not in possession of this guide, please obtain a copy from the Personnel Manager.

Figure 12   An 'MBO-type' appraisal report form

PART 1   PERFORMANCE ASSESSMENT

(a) Summary of performance against objectives listed in Part 2 of previous report, including comment on significant achievements related to key tasks.

_____
_____
_____
_____
_____
_____
_____
_____
_____
_____
_____
_____

(b) List specific actions taken since the last performance appraisal to improve the job-holder's capabilities, detailing the improvements achieved.

_____
_____
_____
_____
_____
_____
_____
_____
_____

Figure 12   An 'MBO-type' appraisal report form (contd)

(c) Performance rating

1 Does not produce an acceptable standard of work

2 Minimally acceptable; requires further training and experience

3 Does not consistently produce a satisfactory standard of performance

4 Achieves a satisfactory standard of performance at all times

5 Has achieved a very high standard of performance at all times

6 Regularly demonstrates outstanding performance

1 2 3 4 5 6

If applicable, indicate specific proposals for improving performance or actioning reassignment.

_____

_____

_____

_____

_____

_____

Figure 12 An 'MBO-type' appraisal report form (contd)

PART 2   FUTURE PERFORMANCE

List *mutually agreed* performance objectives for the forthcoming period.

_____
_____
_____
_____
_____
_____
_____
_____
_____
_____
_____

Detail any required amendments to the employee's job description.

_____
_____
_____
_____
_____

PART 3   RECOMMENDATION FOR PROMOTION

(a) If not recommended for promotion, state reasons.

_____
_____
_____

*Figure 12   An 'MBO-type' appraisal report form
(contd)*

(b) Recommendation for normal promotion:

Recommended (   )   Strongly recommended (   )

Comment _____

_____

(c) Recommendation for special/accelerated promotion

Comment _____

_____

_____

PART 4   FOR COMPLETION BY APPRAISEE

I have discussed my Self-Appraisal Review and this report with my manager and I have the following comments to make _____

_____

_____

_____

_____

_____

_____

_____

Signature of Appraiser _____ Date _____

Signature of Appraisee _____ Date _____

Figure 12   An 'MBO-type' appraisal report form
(contd)

PART 5   COUNTERSIGNING MANAGER'S REPORT

_____

_____

_____

_____

_____

_____

Signed _____   Date _____

Figure 12   An 'MBO-type' appraisal report form (contd)

Having had Figure 12 shoved under your nose, you may feel inclined to agree with my earlier assertion that any truly worthwhile stab at MBO will be intensely time-consuming. To be rudely blunt, it doesn't end there, because we also have to admit that relatively few of us are skilled practitioners in the difficult art of written communication. One has only to glance at paperwork plucked at random from any management cesspool and there it is, our bleeding Achilles' heel – an almost endemic dislike-cum-fear of wielding the written word.

So, a word of warning! If and when you try to convince other managers that MBO-type appraisal is the way ahead, be ready to *analyse* the barrage of excuses and criticism that'll probably come your way. More often than not, this expressed antipathy will be nothing more than a cloak to camouflage their one real worry – the likely chance that the demand for lengthy and thoughtful writing will hoist them high on their own petards of communicational inability.

THE 'NOTES FOR GUIDANCE'

Figure 13 (not unlucky for some, I hope) depicts suggested 'notes for guidance' for use in conjunction with the sample appraisal form. Again, your task, remember, is to utilise them as food for thought.

STAFF CONFIDENTIAL

PLUNKETTS LTD

NOTES FOR GUIDANCE
COMPLETION OF THE STAFF APPRAISAL REPORT

Introduction

Used in conjunction with the Self-Appraisal Review, the Staff Appraisal Report is a key aid to good management within the company. The completed report is designed to present information in a useful form for the purposes of:

- Encouraging frank and open discussion between the manager and the appraisee on the latter's performance during the period under review and his/her goals for the future.
- Helping the manager to identify training needs and make decisions on the job-holder's career development.
- Providing a vehicle for the assessment of promotion potential and/or the implementation of suitable action in cases of inefficiency, etc.

Implementing the appraisal scheme

When implementing the scheme, please ensure that you observe the following sequence of events:

Figure 13   'Notes for guidance' to accompany the appraisal form depicted in Figure 12

1 The job-holder should be provided with a copy of the Self-Appraisal Review for completion *at least fourteen days before the scheduled appraisal discussion.* You should ensure that he/she returns the completed review to you at least two working days before the discussion is due to take place.

2 It is vital to the successful outcome of the job-holder's appraisal that you carefully examine his/her completed Self-Appraisal Review.

PART 1

● Compare the job responsibilities entered by the employee in the first section with those listed in his/her Job Description. Take note of any apparent anomalies for subsequent discussion and mutual resolution.

● Consider any claims made by the employee in the second section relating to job responsibilities not listed in his/her Job Description. Take note of any apparent anomalies for subsequent discussion and mutual resolution.

● Consider the 'percentages of time spent' entered by the employee in both sections, and, again, take note of any anomalies for subsequent discussion and mutual resolution.

PART 2

● Striving for the utmost impartiality, weigh any comments made by the employee in this Part against your own views regarding his/her strengths and weaknesses. Consider with care any alleged organizational or other problems, together with the employee's suggestions for

Figure 13 'Notes for guidance' to accompany the appraisal form depicted in Figure 12 (contd)

overcoming them. Remember that the employee's comments (together with any made in Part 3) should provide you with an indication of his/her stance at the forthcoming appraisal counselling session, and take notes accordingly.

PARTS 3 and 4
● These parts provide an opportunity for the responsible employee to provide you with a reasoned indication of his/her views regarding personal development and plans for the future. Since this topic will be a prime subject for discussion at the appraisal counselling session, you should take full advantage of this 'advance notification' and garner your advice.

Completing the appraisal

(a) Please note that the report form should NOT be completed before the counselling session. Instead, prepare draft notes of your intended comments and assessments, and use these as a basis for your discussion with the appraisee.

(b) Remember that, before you can objectively discuss and assess performance, you must be clear in your own mind what you, as the employee's manager, expect of him/her in terms of specific aims and objectives, and you should strive to obtain mutual agreement on these all-important issues.

Figure 13   'Notes for guidance' to accompany the appraisal form depicted in Figure 12 (contd)

(c) Remember also the several purposes of the appraisal counselling session; namely:

(i) to carry out an in-depth review of the appraisee's performance against *agreed* objectives during the period under report;

(ii) to scrutinize and, where necessary, update his/her job description;

(iii) to solve any personal conflicts or problems;

(iv) to foster and improve the appraisee's motivation to succeed;

(v) to make specific proposals for improving his/her performance by means of training or other experience;

(vi) where relevant, to broach the question of promotion or reassignment;

(vii) to mutually agree challenging but realistic targets for the forthcoming period.

(d) Once the counselling session is over, you should complete the report form and pass it to the subject for his/her consideration and signature. It is most important that you encourage the employee to make written comment in Part 4 of the form, particularly when his/her views are at variance with those expressed in the report.

(e) The report should then be forwarded without delay to the countersigning manager for action.

Figure 13   'Notes for Guidance' to accompany the appraisal form depicted in Figure 12 (contd)

In an ideal world, that would be that. However, since the trail through the appraisal jungle is littered with the skeletons of hapless managers who've come unstuck, I'm afraid there's more to come – after, that is, we've tackled the little question of Work Box Number 4.

Work Box Number 4

Task 1. Since you're supposed to gain at least something from slaving away at these Work Boxes, here's a further pearl to add to your academic knowledge-strands . . . The technique of management by objectives owes everything to the base-rock philosophy originally spawned by those mighty management gurus, Peter Drucker and Douglas McGregor. While Drucker expounded the view that the effective boss should concentrate on motivating his managers to achieve a common goal, McGregor quite rightly trumpeted his Theory Y about people at work, namely, that the vast majority will not only take on but also seek responsibility. And t'was from this fertile seed-bed that MBO sprang – and flourished.

End of lesson . . . But what *is* MBO? Grab your pencil and paper and, without cribbing, come up with a definition of the process.

Task 2. When you commence spreading the MBO gospel (as I hope you will), it's odds on that someone in your team will pose the query, 'Er, yes, but what exactly is it, eh?' So, prepare yourself for the occasion by writing out a more detailed and down-to-earth description of the process.

Well, go on, then – what are you waiting for?

Tutorial to Work Box Number 4

Task 1. One can say that MBO is a process which seeks to integrate the organization's need to establish and achieve its various goals with the individual manager's need to contribute to the corporate effort and, at the same time, develop his own potential. I have no means of knowing exactly what you've noted down, but I expect it's something along those lines. The important thing is, don't cast your definition lightly aside; consider your words with care, and if they make good, sound common sense, remember them.

Task 2. You should have found this little task pretty straightforward. However, in the unlikely event that your description is a bit out of kilter, why, it's back to the drawing-board for a spot of essential revision, isn't it?

MBO is a process whereby managers mutually agree with their seniors the specific objectives of their respective jobs, and express these agreed objectives in terms of targets or standards (where possible, quantified) of performance for key areas of work. To ensure corporate as well as individual development, these personal objectives are aligned with departmental and organizational objectives, and managers are thus made well aware of their contributions to the success or failure of the outfit as a whole. Individual performance is reviewed jointly by the boss and the junior, and, arising from this frank and open discussion, further realistic targets are agreed.

6 On how to avoid disaster

Not many months ago, I was lucky enough to receive an invitation from a medium-sized, high-tech company to advise on the setting up of an appraisal scheme for all their employees – with, of course, the traditional exception of the sacrosanct, we've-arrived-and-to-prove-it-we're-here top brass. Thus it was that, one rainy morning, I sallied forth for my first meeting with my new client; an encounter which, as events turned out, was to be the prelude to my witnessing an appraisal disaster of simply majestic proportions. But I'm leaping ahead. Let me tell you of the lull before the storm, because that's what matters.

On the whole, I found this particular Big Daddy and his senior managers to be a most pleasant and seemingly very efficient bunch. There were five of them at this first meeting and, by the end of the morning, they'd painted an encouraging picture of a well knit, thriving company which, blessed with a stable and eminently capable workforce, was definitely on the up-and-up. At the end of the session I was taken on the usual Cook's Tour of the premises – and, boy, was I impressed! In terms of design, modern décor and general ambience, the so-called production floor looked more like a public library than a place in which things were actually manufactured. The individual, custom-designed work positions were bright and airy, and each section was nicely delineated by open-plan screening – with, believe it or not, a rich array of potted plants providing the finishing touch! True, the work itself (which abounded in silicon chips and other electronic paraphernalia), demanded a high level of cleanliness. But, believe me, this place was a production paradise . . .

Now we come to the crunch. In undertaking the meeting with the firm's senior management (and, most certainly, before daring to suggest that, yes, an appraisal scheme would be beneficial to their needs), I'd set myself the usual and primary task of ensuring to my satisfaction that the organizational climate was not only right but ripe for such a development. To this end, I discussed a range of topics with the MD and his colleagues, which, for your information, I'll now reduce to a dreadfully truncated resumée:

1 *Their 'management style'* The general tenor of the discussion served to convince me that I'd stumbled on an outfit where consultative-cum-participative management was the order of the day. For instance, the managers described in detail and with evident enthusiasm how a policy of Total Quality had been successfully introduced, and I must admit that I was very impressed by their account of the manner in which this process had included in-depth consultation at all levels, including the shop floor.

2 *Communication* I was extremely pleased to gather from that which I heard that the dreaded 'need to know' philosophy just didn't seem to apply in this company. I was told with evident pride how each and every manager and supervisor was committed to keeping his/her respective subordinates fully in the picture, and not just the good news, either – as it was put to me by the MD, the efficient dissemination of information to employees meant 'warts an' all'. I was shown copies of the bi-monthly newsletter which everyone received, and I liked what I saw. I was told of the efforts to utilize notice boards as they should be utilized, and not as graveyards for tatty, dog-eared and deadly uninteresting bits of bumph. Here, I reasoned, was a management that recognized the vital importance of good communication.

3 *Conditions of employment* In addition to paying their people well in line with the going rate, the company

provided first class, heavily subsidized canteen facilities; and, as a further example of its punctilious attention to detail, even the toilets serving the shop floor would have done credit to any hotel establishment. I was therefore not surprised to be told that the labour turnover rate was extremely low, that the vast majority of the employees had been with their employer for over five years, and that there was an unduly high proportion of 'ten-plus' long-servers included within their number.

4 *The working environment* I've already referred to one aspect, so suffice it to add that all the company buildings were modern in design, maintained to a very high standard, and, all in all, constituted the type of workplace which positively motivated people to work happily and well.

So, in the light of this most interesting and rewarding discussion, I had little hesitation in concluding that here, at the very least, was an organization in which a well founded appraisal scheme would not only be welcomed by all and sundry, but would thrive.

Huh, I'm ashamed to admit it, but I couldn't have been more wrong!

Having duly agreed on how the scheme was to be implemented, I turned up several weeks later, all eager and rarin' to go, to conduct the first of several training sessions: to wit, a two-day course on 'Staff Appraisal', directed at the firm's middle managers.

At this point, it's necessary for me to mention that (doubtless, like you, reader) I place great importance on successfully breaking the ice before getting down to the nitty-gritty of any training session – and, although it's meself wot says it, over the years I've developed a mini-arsenal of 'tricks of the trade' that damned near always achieve this laudable aim. But not on this occasion . . .

An hour into the flamin' thing and, despite my best efforts, there they continued to squat, fourteen Jack and Jill Managers

sporting dead-pan, cold fish, pickled-onion-eyed faces –
frigid, icy and utterly unforthcoming. I don't know whether
you've ever been stuck with this kind of situation, but for my
money, and rightly or wrongly, there's only one thing to be
done – and I did it. Throwing caution (and, likely, my fee) to
the winds, I tossed my postcard notes to the table with a
slightly theatrical flourish and uttered something like this:
'Okay, folks, I'm a big boy . . . (it's perhaps fortunate that I
err on the large side) . . . so come on, you miserable lot,
what's gnawing at yer vitals, then?'

Thank heavens, the desperate stratagem worked! The
flood-gates crashed open and I was deluged with a tumultuous
Niagara of complaints and vociferous, well-he-asked-for-it
cries from the heart, of which the following are but a tiny
sample:

'D'you realize, Mr Goodworth, that until you started
talking, WE DIDN'T EVEN KNOW WHY WE WERE
SITTING HERE?'

'Appraisal scheme, d'you say – CAREER DEVELOP-
MENT? What gave you the idea that there's any career
prospects with this lot?'

'They've really been feeding you the gears, haven't they?'

'IMPROVE MORALE? I reckon you'd do well to have a
word with the people on the shop floor – they'd tell you a
thing or two about the morale at this place . . .'

'NOW what are the buggers up to, eh?'

Eventually I managed to stem this rip-tide of emotive
reaction, and then, of course, had to make a decision. I wasn't
the first training wallah to be faced with the big dilemma, and I
know for dead certain I'm not the last: that's to say, if
contracted to present a certain course (as, indeed, I was), what
does one do when faced with such shattering evidence that to
carry on will result in a well-nigh disastrous outcome? You

may agree that there are a few alternative solutions, namely:

(a) adopt the 'it's-their-problem' attitude of the money-skimming, hard nut consultant, and carry on regardless;
(b) kick the whole thing into touch there and then, i.e. dismiss the group and tell whoever's concerned that they're on a hiding to nothing;
(c) having allowed the delegates to blow off steam, attempt to rationalize the situation by getting to the heart of the problem, and then, if there is the slightest chance of success, carry on with one's contracted assignment.

For better or worse, I elected for the last alternative, and, by dint of careful questioning, arrived at the incontrovertible, highly unpalatable truth. My assessment of the company's organization climate had been hopelessly wrong. So, in order that you, reader, may be better equipped to deal with just such a situation, should it ever arise, I'll now spell out the true state of affairs that pertained within this firm:

1 *The 'management style'* So far as the senior managers was concerned, they were rankly and consistently autocratic in their approach. What they'd described in glowing terms as 'consultative sessions' and so on were, in reality, *command meetings*, when, brooking no discussion, they'd bulldozed their way through things and imposed whatever they thought fit on those under them.

2 *Communication* If I'd had the nunce to look closely at the proffered newsletter, if I'd actually gone out of my way to acquaint myself with the make-up and quality of this management's activities in terms of communication; why, I'd have dropped the assignment like a hot potato. The newsletter and sundry other bits of paper were clearly utilized by Big Daddy and his team in much the same way as Dr Goebbels plied his propagandist trade. It was transparently clear that this employer's verbal and written communication was unilateral, uncaring and, again, totally autocratic.

3   *Conditions of employment and the working environment*   No, my eyes hadn't deceived me, everything was first class, but the fact that the majority of employees were long-servers didn't mean that they were a satisfied and contented workforce. Far from it, discontent was rife, and I soon ascertained that damned near everyone below director level had taken the decision to make the most of the excellent conditions, despite their full-blooded and well justified contempt for those at the top.

As for this particular day's 'training', the unscheduled hair-down session did, at least, produce one beneficial effect, in that the proverbial ice had been broken in no uncertain fashion. So, once the delegates had vented their spleen, I was able to get back on track and, taking care to avoid any really contentious issues, managed to keep them moderately alive and interested for the remainder of the time.

That evening I sought out the MD and, using what powers of impartiality I possessed to the full, endeavoured to lay things on the line. The worthy gentleman listened for a few minutes, then, with a testy grimace, said something like, 'Mr Goodworth, it's obvious that you've gained an entirely false impression of our company – and I can only assume that this is because you haven't achieved the right rapport with our managers. I therefore think it would be better for all concerned if we terminated our present arrangement . . .'

I must admit that this royal heave-ho wasn't totally unexpected, but, for all that, I do recall being distinctly peeved as I tackled the long drive homewards.

Some weeks passed and then, out of the blue, I received a telephone call from the company's personnel manager, with whom I'd become quite chummy. Having stressed that what he was about to say was strictly off the record, he told me that the MD had steam-rollered a home-grown appraisal scheme through, down to and including the people on the shop floor. As I remember it, he said, '. . . there's now one holy hell of a shindig going on. The entire workforce is up in arms, and the production operatives have issued an ultimatum that if the appraisal scheme isn't withdrawn, they'll stage a walk-out . . .'

I didn't hear any more from my friendly mole, so that's the end of this particular tale of appraisal disaster, except to express the hope that your reaction is one of 'message received and understood'.

Concluding the all-too-obvious lesson, to scatter the seeds of appraisal in all but the finest of organization climates is to invite, at the very least, a sterile growth – and to sow them in a climate of rampant discontent is to guarantee catastrophe. If he or she has a grain of intelligence, even the most autocratic of managers should acknowledge that, to yield tangibly worthwhile results, appraisal must be conducted on the basis of mutual respect and agreement, NOT by unilateral assessment against a backcloth of fear and distrust on the part of those who undergo the process.

GIVEN A DOLLOP OF LUCK – A RECIPE FOR SUCCESS

Note, if you will, the *caveat* in them thar words. The crux of creating the right bed-rock environment for the introduction of appraisal comprises a three-fold developmental thrust, and, yes, it's wise to remember that Lady Luck will have a significant say in the outcome:

- The sure and certain task of changing the attitudes of some (if not all) of the nominated appraisers;
- Appropriate skills training in appraisal techniques;
- Thorough briefing (and, most likely, more attitude-changing) of those who are to be appraised.

Let's now plonk our size elevens where angels fear to tread and, initially, look at a course syllabus, call it what you will, designed to achieve the first two of these objectives.

TRAINING IN APPRAISAL
(A suitably innocuous title, I think you'll agree)

1 *Introduction*
The aims of the course are outlined and explained.

NOTES
(a) As with all courses, the introduction can make or mar the event. One essential ingredient for success is the calibre of the person presenting the programme. If the personality is wrong, if the ability to break the ice and swiftly achieve rapport with the delegates is conspicuous by its absence, then the thing is virtually doomed from the start. Needless to say, I'm assuming that if you have a hand in organizing the training, you'll ensure that whoever's in the driving seat is fully qualified for the job in terms of knowledge and experience. And don't say, 'That's flamin' obvious', because you and I know that the training world is awash with cowboys and incompetents.
(b) I'd personally recommend that the introduction includes frank and pretty forcible reference to the fact that much of the course will be concerned with highlighting and changing attitudes.

2 *A question of style*
A reminder to delegates by way of graphic description that individuals possess widely disparate management styles – autocratic, paternalistic, diplomatic, consultative-cum-participative, etc. A detailed self-questionnaire designed to illustrate the point, followed by frank and open discussion on the results, will fill the bill.

NOTES
(a) A suitably punchy film is a useful means of ramming home the business of varying management styles.
(b) Regarding the self-questionnaire, there are a number of them currently on the market. Since I have other than philanthropic reasons for being a flippin' author, allow me to make the unblushing comment that my last book, *The Secrets of Successful People Management* (Heinemann – bless them! – 1988) contains just such a self-questionnaire.)
(c) The optimistic aim of the 'frank and open discussion' bit is to persuade those concerned, by hook or by crook, that their revealed attitudes are a deterrent to successful appraisal and to convince them of a need to change their leopards' spots. May the force be with you!

3 *The vexed old game of rating strengths and weaknesses*
Graphic rating scales need to be explained and illustrated. Give an account of the various pitfalls which lurk in the path of the appraiser – 'playing the rating game', the weaknesses of varying standards, central tendency, leniency, halo, systematic and total errors, the need for narrative comment as a justification for ratings, and *vice versa*.

NOTES
(a) Take pity on their aching backsides – remember the soporific affect of overmuch chalk and talk! Make this a participative session with exercises to reinforce the delegates' learning and test their understanding.
(b) When it comes to the bit on narrative comment, remember also that yer average manager is not noted for his or her powers of written expression, and will avoid such work like the plague. Be merciless, task them with producing short, sharp narrative comments on given criteria, and discuss the results in frankly open forum. Such an activity won't provide them with much practice, but it may well provoke them to take an additional pause for thought when it comes to the real thing.

4 *Completing the chosen appraisal documents*
Explanation and use of the Self-Appraisal Review is necesssary (if applicable), i.e. introduction to the 'Notes for Guidance', leading to an explanation and completion of the Appraisal Report itself, and relevant administrative procedures outlined and explained.

NOTE
The session should include an in-depth explanation (with associated discussion) of the qualities required to be rated in each form. If suitably realistic role play exercises can be introduced, all the better.

5 *The vital art of counselling*
Deal with management in interviewing, in general – counselling techniques, handling cases of inadequacy, poor conduct, disagreement, etc.

NOTES TO FOLLOW
Aye, you're right, this is untrodden territory, but never fear – we're going to be up to our ears in counselling in the next chapter.

6 *Course review and open forum*

You'll recall that the third step in preparing the ground for an appraisal scene is concerned with the 'thorough briefing (and, most likely, more attitude-changing) of those to be appraised'. Note my emphasis on the probable need for attitude-changing, and, lest you doubt this, cast your eyes over the following sample of reactions by real-life employees on being told that they were to undergo formal appraisal.

'Tell you what I think, they're going to use the appraisal scheme as an excuse for limiting pay increases . . .' (Comment by a production supervisor with some ten years' service who, rightly or wrongly, had a pretty jaundiced view of his management.)

'Huh, another bloody nine day wonder – what'll they think of next?' (A scornful indictment by a section leader who proceeded to catalogue what he regarded as his employer's past failures to translate umpteen proposals into positive action.)

'We hear what you say, Clive, but how are we going to get a fair deal from our boss? When it comes to dealing with people, he's absolutely hopeless.'

'Can you imagine Eric coping with that – he'd run a mile rather than face one of us across the desk . . .'

'I wouldn't put it past him to say one thing and write another . . .'

'Him appraise us? You must be joking . . .' (A gaggle of reactions from some secretaries who reckoned they knew their admin manager's shortcomings – and probably did.)

'Look, this is all very well, but how do I know that my boss's assessments won't be lower than everyone else's? I mean, how am I going to know whether I'm getting a fair crack of the whip, or not?' (A well-justified comment on varying standards by a junior manager.)

The important point is, it matters little whether such doubts and fears are founded on good, solid evidence or are pure figments of the imagination – their mere existence can spell trouble for any appraisal scheme. Y'know, managements the world over suffer from two near-endemic weaknesses. The first is their inability to see the morale wood for the trees. They fail to recognize that their respective employees have them constantly under a magnifying glass, and that any executive pimples, however minute, are very often seen as festering boils – with consequent dents to morale. The second malaise is the manner in which *heap big* management clangers and trickeries are viewed, if at all, by the perpetrators as having little or no effect on employee relations or morale, in general. This outstanding aptitude for executive myopia is a constant source of frustration and annoyance to subordinates, and, of course, to those who are truly dedicated to managing people effectively and well.

So, the message must be, if you wish to avoid potentially horrendous appraisal troubles, do everything in your power to ensure that the intended appraisees are given extensive briefings, encouraged to voice their doubts and fears, and have them assuaged.

A CHECKLIST FOR BRIEFING APPRAISEES

1 Explain the true purpose(s) of the appraisal scheme – and, just as important, what it will *not* be used for.
2 Emphasize the open, participative nature of the scheme.
3 Acknowledge the inherent weaknesses of any appraisal scheme in terms of the 'human element' (subjectivity, varying standards, etc.), and describe in detail the steps which are being taken to minimize these snags:

(a) the training of appraisers;
(b) the briefing of appraisees;
(c) the 'two-prong approach' – self-appraisal (to be dealt with later in the briefing) and manager's appraisal as a basis for mutual agreement;

    (d) the opportunity for appraisees to comment in writing on the completed report without fear of any form of reprisal;

    (e) the verification, or otherwise, of the report by the appraiser's manager;

    (f) the provision of an appeals procedure (see Chapter 7);

    (g) the institution of an audit of the progress of the scheme as a whole; which, in any event, will be conducted on a pilot basis for the first twelve months (again, see Chapter 7).

4 Provide an in-depth explanation of the make-up and completion of the Self-Appraisal Review and Staff Appraisal Report.

5 Encourage questions – and jolly well answer them!

If there's one thing in appraisal that managers fear more than completing the report itself, it's the eyeball-to-eyeball appraisal discussion, and that's what we are going to examine in the next chapter. But, before we do that, there is the little matter of Work Box Number 5 to be completed, isn't there?

Work Box Number 5

Task 1. A senior personnel manager has introduced a staff appraisal scheme which comprises numerical assessment of given abilities/qualities by means of six-point graphical rating scales. Having received some 250 completed reports, he wishes to gain a *broad* indication as to whether or not the composite ratings in respect of 'Performance' tend to reflect the error of leniency on the part of the appraisers concerned.

Since we haven't touched on this particular topic, you may deem it an unfair question – but here it is, anyway. How can the personnel manager set about achieving his aim?

Task 2. Make critical comment on the following completed sections of a mythical appraisal report.

- -

STAFF CONFIDENTIAL

The Phlum-Lump Cough Candy Co Ltd

STAFF APPRAISAL REPORT

Name Charles Bloggs   *Appointment* Office Supervisor
Period of Report 1987–8   *Appraised by* T. B. Long

PERFORMANCE

	High						Low
Knowledge of job	7	6	5	④	3	2	1
Attendance	7	6	⑤	4	3	2	1
Punctuality	7	6	⑤	4	3	2	1
Team management	7	6	5	④	3	2	1
Good housekeeping	7	6	5	4	③	2	1

Comments Charlie has a good overall knowledge of his job and maintains a fair control over the personnel in his charge. So far as the latter ability is concerned, this was particularly apparent during the complications of the recent organizational changes. I am unable to fault his attendance and punctuality, and only wish that certain aspects of his personality were as satisfactory, in which event he would make a first-rate supervisor.

PERSONALITY

	High					Low	
Co-operation	7	6	5	4	3	②	1
Dependability	7	6	⑤	4	3	2	1
Initiative	7	6	5	4	③	2	1
Adaptability	7	6	5	④	3	2	1
Leadership qualities	7	6	5	4	③	2	1

Comments Although industrious and a dependable worker, Charlie's highly developed sense of individuality does little to help his attitude to his seniors, which can be very annoying. He must learn that loyalty to his employer embraces the need for respect for the wishes of his seniors, and that his personal brand of abrasiveness does little to foster these vital relationships.

SUITABILITY FOR PROMOTION

High   Low
7 6 5 4 3 ② 1

Comments Not ready or qualified for promotion, as yet.

- -

Tutorial to Work Box Number 5

Task 1. As I'm sure you twigged, if the personnel manager plots all the composite ratings for 'Performance' according to their distribution on the six-point scale, he will then be in a position to see whether the results represent anything like a normal probability curve. Broadly speaking, for a six-point scale, the yardstick is as depicted in Figure 14.

Approximately 2% of all appraisees merit a rating of 6

Approximately 14% of all appraisees merit a rating of 5

Approximately 34% of all appraisees merit a rating of 4

Approximately 34% of all appraisees merit a rating of 3

Approximately 14% of all appraisees merit a rating of 2

Approximately 2% of all appraisees merit a rating of 1

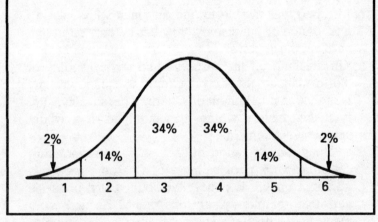

Figure 14   Percentage of appraisees falling in each portion of a normal distribution on a six-point scale

Task 2. Mr Long's appraisal efforts on behalf of the Phlum-Lump Cough Candy Company have not been helped by the choice of a seven-rating scale. That said, he's certainly not improved matters by his pretty ropey choice of narrative comment, which is either irrelevant to the appraisal section concerned or fails to justify his numerical ratings (or, as we've noted several times before, *vice versa*). To be more specific, his naughties include the following:

(a) His assessment of 'fair' in respect of team management neither sits easily with his rating of '4', nor does it really accord with his further comment on Charlie's performance during the 'recent organizational changes'. With regard to the former point, how can he equate a rating of '4' to 'good' (job knowledge) and, in the same breath, equate it to 'fair' (control over personnel)?

(b) If Long was unable to find any fault with Charlie's attendance or punctuality, why has he only rated him as '5' on these items?

(c) In finishing off his narrative under the heading of 'Performance', the silly buffer has quite wrongly launched into comment on Charlie's personality, and, to make matters worse, has indulged in a wildly subjective statement.

(d) Plainly, Long's rating of '2' for 'Co-operation' indicates his very poor opinion of Charlie where this personal quality is concerned, but, really, does his narrative comment justify this rating? He makes no mention of *specific instances* when Charlie failed to co-operate, and he fails to go into detail regarding the employee's alleged 'attitude to his seniors', 'lack of respect' or 'personal brand of abrasiveness'.

(e) Phlum-Lump's poor judgement in requiring their appraisers to rate 'Suitability for Promotion' on a seven-point scale hasn't exactly helped Long.

However, faced with this requirement, he would have been well advised to compile a more detailed justification for his rating of '2', e.g. the length of time Charlie had been in his present post and precisely why he was neither ready nor qualified for promotion.

Who knows, you may well have come up with some further observations – in which case, be your own discerning critic, and pronounce, accordingly!

7 The nitty-gritty of appraisal counselling

I'd like to set the scene for this chapter by throwing a wee gauntlet at your feet. If you're not a betting person, forgive me while I carry on, regardless. Whenever you find yourself chatting to a manager-colleague, create a few ripples by posing this simple question: 'Mary, forgive my curiosity, have you ever had any training in interviewing techniques?'

'I'll wager that on nearly every such occasion, the response will be something like this: 'Er, none, actually. Why d'you ask?'

From time to time, you'll almost certainly detect a defensive note in the reply: 'None – but, y'know, I've had several years' experience at the game . . .'

Now you know what's coming . . . Yet another author-cum-trainer is about to perform his voice-in-the-wilderness bit and rudely lambast you with the cry, 'Call yourself an interviewer? In a pig's ear, you are . . .' All of which is a fairly dodgy way to win friends and influence people, so I'd better dish up a shred or two of evidence to justify such impertinence.

Well, if there was such a thing as an international league table for interviewing prowess, there's precious little doubt that British managers would figure mightily low on the list. Normally, I don't place a great deal of faith in statisticians, but I'll defend one of their assertions to the hilt; namely, that of all the managers in our midst who are required to interview people, only around a miserable 3 per cent have received any worthwhile training in the art. In digesting this fact (aye, for my money, it's a fact, and you'd better believe it!), note my reference to *worthwhile* training. That was a deliberate choice of adjective, because there's no way that the odd half-day's training in interviewing techniques will induce more than a vague familiarization with the ground rules of the game.

Pushing these dire observations a stage further, it takes a good one-and-a-half days to inculcate trainees with the principles and practice of *basic interviewing*, and a further couple of days, minimum, to make them even near-proficient in any of the *specialist* areas, say:

(a) selection interviewing;
(b) disciplinary interviewing;
(c) interrogating;
(d) welfare counselling;

and, wait for it!

(e) *appraisal counselling*.

Eureka, my task is quite clear – in order to make myself shine in your eyes, I've simply got to make this chapter the instructive and entertaining equivalent of several days' intensive training . . . Huh, I'll tell you now, IT WON'T WORK. If you really wish to become an effective appraisal counsellor, you'll utilize what follows as nothing more than a kid's primer, and, then, having learned your ABC, get yourself on a proper course of practical training. Take my word for it, you deserve and require nothing less.

WHY APPRAISAL COUNSELLING IS 'DIFFERENT'

In order to highlight why the techniques of appraisal counselling differ from other forms of interviewing, let's conduct a mini-analysis of three types of interviewing situations:

- THE INTERROGATION
- THE SELECTION INTERVIEW
- THE APPRAISAL COUNSELLING SESSION

First, one aspect of the INTERROGATION. In this type of 'When-did-you-last-see-your-father?' confrontation, the entire thing is *highly controlled*, i.e. the subject is allowed precious little latitude to take the initiative during the session. Jack or Jill is there to be grilled, and grilled he or she will be.

In the SELECTION INTERVIEW, it can be said that the style of an efficiently conducted session occupies the middle position on the scale of control, i.e. it is *covertly planned or phased*.

Whereas, when we come to the APPRAISAL COUN-SELLING SESSION, we find that the overall style has zoomed way out to the other end of the scale, i.e., it is *virtually uncontrolled*. Figure 15 sets out to illustrate its essential features.

Plainly, no single *modus operandi* is appropriate to all interview situations. The trick is to recognize the different styles and techniques, and to utilize that which is appropriate to the purpose of the interview and the personality of the interviewee. When it comes to questioning techniques, this does not mean to say that the interviewer should stick like glue to a particular method (for example, it is almost always necessary to pose a few direct questions during any type of interview), but, rather, that the tenor of the session should reflect the appropriate style.

Moreover, and this is extremely important, *the would-be appraisal counsellor should note the extent to which his or her personality will be characterized by the type of questions posed*, and, thus, make or mar a counselling session. Take a long, hard look at Figure 16.

NON-INTERROGATIVE *(Appraisal Counselling)*	PLANNED/ PHASED *(Selection)*	INTERROGATIVE (Discipline)
1 THE INTERVIEWER'S FUNCTION		
Is that of the counsellor	Is that of the conversation guide	Is that of the interrogator
2 RELATIONSHIP WITH INTERVIEWER		
Is that of helper and adviser	Is that of friendly 'equality'	Is that of boss/ junior
3 DEGREE OF CONTROL EXERTED BY INTERVIEWER		
Minimal	Some covert	Explicit
4 PRIMARY CHARACTERISTIC OF SESSION		
Open/freeranging	Flexibility	Rigidity
5 THE PATTERN OF THE SESSION		
Open-ended 'prompters' and many reflectback questions	Mainly openended with some reflect-back questions	Many direct and leading questions
The counsellor supports the appraisee, builds upon replies, and waits out pauses	The interviewer conducts a carefully steered conversation	The interrogator sets the pace, probes and interrupts at will

Figure 15 The appraisal counselling session highlighted

HIGHLY CONTROLLED MODE

Direct questions
Questions that provoke short and generally un-profitable responses, like 'Yes' and 'No', e.g.

Did you break into the locker?
Do you admit that you lied?
Is that all you have to say?

Leading or standard-revealing questions
Questions that prompt an interviewee to make hoped-for responses, e.g.

Honesty is always the best policy – now, why did you start this fight?
You have admitted that you were present at the time the offence was committed, so give me one good reason why you should not be charged with theft.
This job entails a goodly amount of overtime. Tell me, how d'you feel about working overtime?

Figure 16   The association between interview style and types of question posed

Steering questions
Questions that induce the interviewee to stick to a desired theme or subject, e.g.

Thanks for telling me about the difficulties at your last job. Now, you started to describe how these affected your work . . .
Just a minute, what happened then?
I think your first point is crucial. Tell me more about that.

PLANNED OR PHASED MODE
(A STEERED CONVERSATION)

Probing questions
Questions that, building upon an earlier response, probe a particular subject, e.g.

Exactly why did you find working with Mr Jones so difficult?
You say the deadline was the tenth of the month. How often did you fail to meet it?
I see – and who was responsible for that?

Figure 16 The association between interview style and types of question posed (contd)

Open-ended questions
Questions that encourage lengthy and informative responses, e.g.

How did that situation come about?
Tell me, how would you sum up your relative strengths and weaknesses as a manager?
Why do you believe that is so?

Reflect-back questions
Questions that 'restate an earlier reply', testing earlier responses and basic attitudes, etc., e.g.

You said that your main difficulty is with the coding. But how can you be so certain? Autocratic, eh? Tell me more!
But earlier, you said you weren't interested in that . . .

NON-CONTROLLED MODE

Figure 16   The association between interview style and types of question posed (contd)

Having established, as it were, the basic framework of the appraisal counselling session, I think it now behoves us to consider some aspects of the process in greater detail.

THE ROLE OF THE APPRAISAL COUNSELLOR

While we're on the subject of individual management styles, let's get one thing absolutely straight. The role of the appraisal counsellor is exactly what it says – that of counsellor. The manager who regards this vitally important function as just another discursive task in his daily round, to be conducted in exactly the same manner as all his other get-togethers, is on a hiding to nothing. If the outcome of any appraisal counselling session is to be crowned with success, the normal, day-to-day boss–subordinate relationship must be shoved into the background; for, however much it may go against the executive grain, counselling is all about *helping*. Therefore, if (and, be it noted, I say *if*) you happen to be cast in the wrought iron mould of someone who can't even conceive of the idea of 'relaxing off' in front of a subordinate, why, you're in dead trouble, and a pretty poor manager, to boot.

What's that? Ah, I hear you. Since you're habitually kind and considerate in your dealings with juniors, you consider this particular mini-diatribe to be superfluous . . . Fair enough, but, being beastly frank, would your people go along with your confident assertion? Would they, for instance, agree wholeheartedly that you're a manager who:

1 Can stop 'emanating authority' at will?
2 Possesses more than an adequate dollop of the human touch?
3 Can listen without interrupting?
4 Can be a helpful friend?

It's all these qualities that, in sum, require the effective manager-counsellor to be something of a chameleon in order to bring 'em off. The question is, are you *really* up to this demanding role? And what about the other managers who'll be taking part in any planned appraisal – are *they* all up to the mark?

THE COUNSELLING ENVIRONMENT

You know what I'm going to say, because you've heard it all before. All interviews, and especially appraisal counselling sessions, should be conducted in a relaxing, encouraging environment . . . Yeah, yeah, yeah, and there you are, stuck with an unattractive, tatty-at-the-edges cell of an office which isn't even a credit to your precious status, let alone near-suitable for counselling! I don't care! If you are realistically contemplating appraisal, you MUST ensure, come hell or high water, that suitable accommodation is always available for counselling – preferably with easy chairs and nothing more than a coffee table as the dividing line. Be warned, the manager who is loath to abandon that psychological fortress, his desk, is very likely to have fooled himself where those counsellor-qualities are concerned.

Now, you shouldn't need reminding that appraisal counselling is by no means immune to the vagaries of our old friend, Murphy's Law, so let's consider some of the more likely contingencies.

COPING WITH THE UNFORTHCOMING APPRAISEE

Picture the scene. You've completed your report (if you're ultra-cautious, probably in pencil) and the time has come for Bertie Entwhistle to attend your presence, with his completed Self-Appraisal Review clutched in his hot little hand – all fired-up and enthusiastic for the fray. 'Tis but a few seconds after you have persuaded him to sit down that you realize you've a lump of well-nigh speechless, wet dough on your hands . . . What d'you do, chum?

Well, first, because you're the guy's boss, you will have

made it your business to get to know him, and, among many other things, you'll know whether this oyster-like behaviour is typical of the creature or not. If it is, you should have been prepared for it, shouldn't you? But, prepared or not, there is a drill that, if you are lucky, will strike a wee spark of rapport:

- Establish in your own mind the cause of Entwhistle's hang-up. Is he basically shy and tongue-tied, or is this a symptom (or a direct flamin' result . . .) of some management fall-down on your part? In other words, does he harbour feelings of resentment, fear or what-all? If the cause is anything but innate shyness, you shouldn't be holding the session until you've done your level best to resolve whatever is wrong. From here on in, we'll assume that shyness is the cause.
- In setting up your counselling sessions, consider the question of seating arrangements. For example, will Entwhistle really feel encouraged when subjected to your basilisk-type glare across the desk, or, just perhaps, would he feel more at home if you both occupied those easy chairs in the corner? And, incidentally, if you haven't been blessed with such outright luxury as a couple of easy chairs, then borrow some luckier soul's office for your counselling.
- An obvious but, nevertheless, tricky step – do all in your power to break the ice:

'Before we kick off, Bert, how did things go with the pigeons on Saturday? When I saw what the weather was like, I thought of your birds struggling their hearts out in that gale – how did they get on, eh?'

'Hey, Bert, you're a bit of an ace with car mechanics, aren't you? I'd much appreciate a spot of advice . . .'

'Sit down, Bert . . . Before we get cracking on our discussion, did you have any trouble completing the Self-Appraisal? I reckon it's the most difficult job of all – how did you find it? . . . Really? That's most interesting – how come? . . . Hey, yes, I'd like to hear more about that . . .'

- Do your level best to avoid posing direct questions, and, instead, concentrate on the 'Magic Six' formula:

  What . . . ?   Where . . . ?   Why . . . ?   Which . . . ?
  Who . . . ? How . . . ?

  'WHAT d'you think were the most interesting features of that particular task?'

  'WHAT are advantages of that approach, d'you think?'

  'WHERE d'you reckon you went wrong?'

  'But WHERE's the disadvantage in that?'

  'WHY was that, d'you think?'

  'Tell me, Bert, WHY d'you think you were asked to complete this Self-Appraisal?'

  'WHICH aspect appealed to you most?'

  'Tell me again – WHICH one was that?'

  'In your view, WHO . . . ?'

  'Of the two juniors, WHO d'you reckon . . . ?'

  'HOW did that come about?'

  'HOW did you set about tackling that aspect?'

- In dragging the Berts of this world out of themselves, it's always a good idea to devote the first chunk of the counselling session to their *good* points. Most folk much prefer discussing their relative strengths rather than their relative weaknesses. (By the way, note that term, 'relative', won't you – it didn't slip in by accident.)

COPING WITH THE YES-MAN

An appraisee who tends to agree too quickly with everything is either a weakling by nature (and you should have recognized this individual trait long before the counselling session reared its head), or is simply anxious to get the whole damned shebang over as quickly as possible. In the latter case, it's advisable to quietly determine the appraisee's motives for acting thus, and, by that, I do *not* mean firing some blockbuster question like, 'All right, then, why are you in such a flickering hurry to get this thing over?'

Keep your ears and eyes open. Is it, for example, the 'critical' aspect that is getting at the appraisee? In other words, is this junior hoping that, by readily agreeing with your comments on relative weaknesses, there will be an escape from lengthy criticism or pontification?

A good general approach to this particular counselling problem is to make the appraisee do all the work.

'Ah, so you agree with me – but, why, precisely?'

'I see you're nodding your head, but, tell me, why d'YOU think I'm justified in expressing that view?'

'And now we come to the question of your competence with the D.14 equipment. How would you rate yourself, and why?'

And if it really comes to the crunch:

'Thus far in our discussion, you've tended to merely agree with everything I've said. Now, let's start afresh . . . I'd like to hear your detailed views on your . . . That's interesting, but WHY, exactly? . . . Fine, but WHY?'

In such situations, once you feel that a fair measure of genuine agreement has been extracted from the appraisee, the discussion can be steered to the question of future objectives and what-not. Again, ensure that it's not you who does all the work:

> 'Right, now I'd like you to consider your personal objectives for the forthcoming year . . . Take so-and-so, for example, what d'you think would be a fair, attainable objective?'

It's worth adding that there's a particular brand of manager who likes nothing better than the appraisee who bends over backwards to agree with everything that's said. Firstly, of course, it's a marvellous sop to the creature's ego when someone is plainly eager to agree with his various and oft-wrong pronouncements, and, secondly, such slavish acquiescence is a sure-fire help in getting the flamin' session over and done with in no time flat. If either cap happens to fit, reader . . .

MANAGING APPRAISAL DISAGREEMENT

Sooner rather than later, you're bound to encounter the appraisee who, probably for very good reason, will have the temerity to disagree with your sterling views on his or her performance, or what-have-you. I've penned those words, 'probably for very good reason', quite deliberately, for in all such instances your first move must be to check the validity of the claim:

> 'Ah, you obviously feel quite strongly on this point . . . Now, tell me frankly, why d'you feel as you do?'

> 'Yes, Tom, I'm beginning to see what you're getting at, but what I'd really like you to do is justify your view. Then, of course, I can give it some serious consideration . . . Now, take your time. Why, exactly, d'you disagree with what I've said?'

> 'So, what you are saying is that . . .' (reflect-back ploy).

'Uh-huh . . . Tell me more about . . .' (probing the grounds for the disagreement).

Having established all there is to know about the reasons for the disagreement, it is then up to you to decide, fairly and squarely, whether or not the arguments you've heard are sufficiently valid to make you change your mind; or, if you're still in honest doubt, to require you to reconsider the issue concerned. If, at the end of the day and despite your best, unprejudiced efforts, the matter cannot be mutually resolved – why, there's only one thing to do. Persuade the appraisee without so much as a trace of rancour to record his or her views in the section of the report form expressly reserved for that purpose, not forgetting to add that the entry will receive careful and impartial consideration 'up the ladder'.

And NEVER forget to ensure that it does.

Work Box Number 6

Study the interview questions that follow, and just for the hell of it, tag each one with the appropriate label from the following:

Direct.
Leading/standard-revealing.
Steering.
Probing.
Open-ended.
Reflect-back.

1   Tell me, how did you gain this experience?
2   Would you say that you are ambitious for leadership?
3   But, if that's the case, why were your figures wrong?
4   You say that you think some further training would be of help. Tell me more about this.
5   Are you certain about this?
6   Why are you so certain about this?
7   I think what you said just now about the system being faulty is very relevant. Where d'you think it breaks down?
8   So, you have difficulty coping with the one-off orders. Is that what you're saying, or have I got it wrong?
9   I reckon that any manager in your position should make a point of qualifying within the first twelve months. Now, what progress have you made to date?
10 Do you consider yourself to be an averagely good communicator?
11 Do you consider yourself to be an averagely good communicator – or what?

12 How would you describe your abilities as a communicator?

13 Why is that, d'you think?

14 Would you say that you're primarily motivated by money?

15 But, just now, you said you weren't keen on figure work . . .

16 Look, I think we've got to resolve this one – so, what's it going to be, eh?

17 There's no doubt that this new appointment will entail a great deal of travel. How d'you feel about that?

18 Tell me, how d'you feel about the prospect of travelling a great deal?

19 I'm glad you've described the difficulties you encountered. Now, you started to tell me about the manner in which they affected your work . . .

20 And which was that?

21 Who was responsible for that part of the job?

22 So, if I understand you correctly, you reckon that the discounts are all wrong . . .

23 Is it possible that somebody in the team has the potential to take this on?

24 Why not?

25 Well, I reckon we've gone through everything in pretty fine detail. Are you happy with the outcome?

Tutorial to Work Box Number 6

Here are my answers to compare with your own.

1 A good, open-ended question that should prompt a worthwhile response.
2 A nastily direct question – and, to some, rude and/or intimidating, to boot.
3 Probing, with more than a touch of the interrogative tar-brush.
4 A handy type of reflect-back question, testing the earlier response.
5 Just maybe, this question is occasionally warranted, but it's 'orribly direct.
6 And this is the far better, open-ended version, as I'm sure you twigged.
7 A combination of reflect-back and probing.
8 A reflect-back attempt which has been spoiled by the implant of a direct question at t'end.
9 Standard-revealing and, given the right kind of sly-boots appraisee, simply asking for an inventedly pleasing response.
10 Hellishly direct – and hopeless.
11 Still hellishly direct, despite the miserable attempt to open-ending the beast.
12 Aha, at long last, beautifully open-ended!
13 Again, nicely open-ended.
14 But this one puts us back in the slammer – direct as one can get.
15 Reflect-back with a smidgin' of probing.
16 If this one is anything but an expression of growing impatience, I reckon it has to be a steering question.
17 Naughtily standard-revealing.
18 And here, of course, is the goodie-type open-ended version.
19 A steering question.
20 Short, succinct, and open-ended.

21 By now, you should be familiar with the Magic Six formula for composing open-ended questions – How?, Why?, What?, Who?, Where?, When? So, once again, this one is nicely open-ended.
22 Reflect-back.
23 This example is infected with the direct question bug – remember Who . . . ?
24 An even shorter one, and still fully open-ended.
25 Huh, a final fling at throwing the direct question gauntlet at the hapless victim's feet.

Cheer up, we're nearing the end of this particularly rocky road. All we've got to do now is take a pretty cool peep at what I choose to call the 'vital after-measures' of appraisal. So, keep your boots on for a final romp, eh?

8 The vital after-measures

The purpose of this final broadside is to convince you, as if 'twere necessary, that it doesn't matter a tinker's cuss to what lengths one goes in cooking up the best appraisal form since sliced bread IF, at one and the same time, the accompanying administrative set-up completely ignores the vital after-measures; to wit, the creation of:

(a) an effective appeals procedure;
(b) a comprehensive system of audit.

So, with the winning post now in sight, let's tackle these last two hurdles.

MAY IT PLEASE YOU, M'LUD, I WISH TO APPEAL

Many companies (but even in this day and age, by no means all of them) boast some form of written disciplinary procedure; and if one looks hard at most of these multifarious attempts to stay on the right side of the law, it's a fair chance that one's eyes will light on a tersely worded paragraph detailing the procedure whereby the odd unfortunate so-and-so can appeal against sentence. Now, if that strikes you as cynical, friend, so be it. The bald truth is, the age-old principle of natural justice may prevail within our legal system, but, in the dubious confines of the company court-room, it's all too often conspicuous by its absence, ousted and supplanted by that devilish, unspoken creed, 'In matters of disciplinary appeal, the gaffer shall obey the rules of the club and do everything possible to prevent his manager looking like a prize chump'. Lest you still condemn my cynicism, think on't – and call to mind the countless occasions when, following his rejection of an appeal, Big Daddy then speaks to his manager-minion along such well-worn lines as:

> 'Look, Carruthers, I've backed your decision – but, quite frankly, you placed me in some difficulty . . . For goodness sake, do try to get these matters more cut-and-dried in the future . . .'

> 'Why the devil did you let things get to the point where he made an appeal? If you'd tackled the matter correctly in the first place, I wouldn't have been forced to back what I regard as pretty poor judgement on your part . . .'

And so on – y'know it happens, even if it is elsewhere.

By now, the point I'm going to make will be staring you in the face, but I intend to press on, regardless.

All, repeat, all appraisal schemes must embody an appeals procedure, and, to coin a phrase, if justice is to be done, *it must be seen to be done*. In the almost certain event that Tom, Dick, Mary or Harriet contests anything within an appraisal, to the point that discussion is of no avail in resolving the issue, then the appraisee should be positively encouraged to invoke the appeals procedure. And, since the world is full of management-scallywags, I'd better add that the discussion should NOT be steered by the appraiser with the single aim of preventing an appeal being lodged; for, as you will have gathered, such a cowardly tactic would simply kick the entire process into touch.

One topic that sometimes causes some head-scratching is the question of who within the outfit should be the arbiter in appraisal appeals. A fairly popular view is that it should be someone who can be said to be 'independent', i.e. for want of a better definition, an executive who is outside the chain of command. Thus and not unnaturally, it is frequently the case that the poor old personnel manager gets clobbered with the chore, although what happens when a member of *his* bailiwick decides to appeal is often left to the gods to decide.

What is imperative is that whoever is selected as arbiter must be an individual who, whatever the circumstances, will remain utterly impartial, *and possess the rare quality of convincing any appellant of that utter impartiality*. Just for the record, how many managers d'you have of that ilk in your organization, excluding yourself, of course?

THE DREADED BUT VITAL BUSINESS OF AUDITING THE BEAST

Once an appraisal scheme has been designed and implemented, what steps should be taken to improve and maintain the quality of the appraisals? What d'you think should be done to discover and recognize their undoubted limitations and deficiencies, and, of course, to overcome these shortcomings? Well, answers to these vexed questions range from a simple, 'Nothing at all, m'dear', to erudite and horribly elaborate procedures of analysis, specialized research, regular revision, and frequent Walpurgis Night purges among the ranks of the appraisers. As you'll have guessed, the 'nothing at all' approach is definitely out. Any appraisal scheme which is just left to tick on of its own volition will, at best, rapidly wither and rot – and, at much more common worst, precipitate a well deserved explosion of criticism and resentment from those who've had the misfortune to suffer under it. So, let's get a realistic after-measures show on the road.

Training
Yes, I know, we've already dealt with this topic in Chapter 6, and I hope you agree that any manager worthy of the name will ensure that everyone, particularly the appraisers, should be subjected to intensive and effective training/briefing before an appraisal scheme swings into operation. But it doesn't end there. Research over the years has demonstrated that regular

training of appraisers will improve resulting appraisals, or, at the very least, prevent an otherwise inevitable deterioration of standards. With the best will in the world, I should add that the company training-officer-cum-manager may not be the ideal choice for delivering the exacting and very specialized form of training; if only for the reason that, by virtue of having already rubbed shoulders with the other managers in the outfit, such worthies will tend to be under the personality-thumb of this and that more forceful colleague. Remember, in this context, that training in appraisal is concerned with changing those leopards' spots, and keeping them changed. Personally, I'd always seek the help of a recognized outside agency for this extremely knotty job.

The ongoing audit of validity and standardization

At the risk of insulting your intelligence, I'm going to kick off each of these topics with a definition:

> *Validity* In short, the requirement that each and every component part of the appraisal form actually achieves what it is intended to achieve. In other words, however much your beautifully designed form impressed you and everyone else at the outset, there needs to be a regular check of the thing in actual use. Are all the instructions, requirements, etc relevant, unambiguous, and producing what you intended them to produce?

> *Standardization* In the context of appraisal, the all-important requirement (see Chapter 3) that standards between appraisers are not subject to unacceptable variance, i.e., that Manager Smith's interpretation of a rating of '4' will be the same as Manager Brown's, that Manager White will place the same interpretation on the term 'good' as Manager Black, and so on. Note also that an unpleasant phenomenon called 'inter-departmental differences' (arising from variances in management style, squabbles, strained relationships, petty jealousies, etc.) can precipitate variations in the standards applied to ratings and assessments.

The business of checking standardization is primarily achieved by combing through all the reports in successive appraisal rounds. The auditor will be on the look-out for such variances as I've mentioned above, and will also keep an eagle eye open for marked changes in the successive reports on specific individuals, ascertaining whether or not they are warranted.

In all probability, you'll have twigged that it takes a rattling good expert to bring off any measure of success with this knotty duo, and, once again, I'd strongly recommend the use of a reputable outside agency.

Make your first round of appraisal a try-out
Whatever the planned frequency of your elected scheme, regard the first complete round as nothing but a trial run. Even if it means that a year or more must pass before the scheme can be utilized for its intended purposes, tell everyone (particularly the appraisees) that the pilot will only be used as a means of sorting out the hiccups that are pretty well bound to occur.

POSTSCRIPT – OR A KIND OF LAST AND ONGOING WORK BOX

If ever you are in the position of planning or influencing the implementation of an appraisal scheme, here's a Priority One task for your attention. Cast your eyes around your organization! Life being what it is, you're pretty well bound to come up with a manager or three who, given all the tuition and brain-washing in the world, will never, ever alter their 'orrible ways . . . On the one hand, your firm may be saddled with examples of the wee timorous beastie-type who couldn't say boo to a goose, let alone conduct a worthwhile appraisal. On the other hand, it may well be cursed with the presence of the odd 24-carat, true-blue autocrat – the type who prefers to eat employees for breakfast, rather than appraise them. So, having noted the presence of these beauties, what d'you do?

It's all right, I'm going to tell you, anyway. Like it or not, you move heaven and earth to ensure that they're not allowed to come within miles of your scheme, because if they are permitted to besmirch it with their widely disparate venoms, it'll die on you. And if it does die, the likelihood is that your organizational climate will suffer one hell of a depression, if not a tempest, in terms of lowered morale.

I'm well aware that, unless one occupies a very senior seat in the plan of things, it takes courage to do what I urge; but did no one ever tell you that one of the prime requirements of efficient crunch-management is pure and simple guts? Rubbing the salt in, ask yourself how often have you been forced to endure the shortcomings of a mismanager-boss, and suffered hell, accordingly? Why should others suffer in like fashion, just because one more would-be member of that miscreant army decides to opt for the easy, mustn't-make-waves life? 'Tis unpalatable food for thought – *and action.*

I wish you all good fortune with your apraisals. 'Bye, now!

Appendix 1

ADDITIONAL COPIES OF TYPICAL RATING
ASSESSMENT APPRAISAL DOCUMENTATION

STAFF CONFIDENTIAL

Name _____

Job Title _____

Dept _____

Review Period _____

**PLUNKETTS LTD
SELF-APPRAISAL REVIEW**

NOTES FOR YOUR GUIDANCE

This self-appraisal review is intended to achieve a number of objectives:

(a) to provide a framework for the forthcoming discussion with your manager;

(b) to enable you to assess your overall performance during the period under review;

(c) to enable you to highlight any additional training which you may feel you require in order to perform your job more effectively;

(d) to help you and your manager to reach agreement on any personal aims which you may seek to achieve during the coming year.

In the event that you have any queries regarding the completion of this review, please do not hesitate to seek the advice of your manager.

A SELF-ASSESSMENT OF YOUR 'PEOPLE-MANAGEMENT SKILLS'

Please consider your current performance in terms of the abilities listed below. Utilizing the scales provided, you are asked to assess your existing level of competence in each ability by circling the appropriate number. Kindly justify each assessment by commenting in the space provided.

1 The ability to manage your team by earning their respect, organizing decisively and inspiring them to greater effort

| I am confident that I organize and inspire my team to give of their best | >>>>>> 6 5 4 3 2 1 <<<<<< | I know that I am inefficient in the use of my team; I engender low morale |

Comment _____

_____

_____

Can you think of any training that would improve your competence in this area? Brief comment, please.

_____

_____

2 Competence in appraising the actual and potential performance of your team members, discussing with each member his/her personal strengths and weaknesses, and counselling with tact and good judgement

I am confident in   >>>>>>   I lack the ability
my   complete   to   carry   out
ability to carry 6 5 4 3 2 1   effective
out   effective   appraisal   and
appraisal   and   <<<<<<   counselling
counselling

Comment _____

_____

_____

Can you think of any training that would improve
your competence in this area? Brief comment,
please.

_____

_____

3 **The ability to handle all disciplinary and grievance matters with the necessary degree of
fairness, firmness and patience.**

I am confident   >>>>>>   I am unable to
that I handle   handle   these
these   matters 6 5 4 3 2 1   matters in the
exactly in the   manner   de-
manner   de-   <<<<<<   scribed
scribed

Comment _____

_____

_____

Can you think of any training that would improve
your competence in this area? Brief comment,
please.

_____

_____

4 The ability to actively develop the work skills and knowledge of all members of your team by identifying individual training needs, implementing or arranging the required training, and maintaining adequate training records.

I am confident   >>>>>>   I am unable to
that I carry out   carry out these
these functions 6 5 4 3 2 1 functions with
with regular and   any degree of
eminent   suc-   <<<<<<   success
cess

Comment_____
_____
_____

Can you think of any training that would improve your competence in this area? Brief comment, please.

_____
_____

5 A full understanding of the positive motivation of people at work and the ability to create and maintain the right conditions for it

Yes, I am a con-   >>>>>>   I do not possess
sistently   effec-   this understand-
tive and excel- 6 5 4 3 2 1 ing or this ability
lent motivator

                      <<<<<<

Comment_____
_____
_____

Can you think of any training that would improve your competence in this area? Brief comment, please.

_____

_____

A SELF-ASSESSMENT OF YOUR 'RESOURCE-MANAGEMENT' SKILLS

6   The ability to make full and economic use of all machinery, equipment and materials within your control

I am confident	>>>>>>	I do not possess
that I am a fully		the ability to
proficient man-	6 5 4 3 2 1	effectively man-
ager of the re-		age the re-
sources within	<<<<<<	sources within
my control		my control

Comment_____

_____

_____

Can you think of any training that would improve your competence in this area? Brief comment, please.

_____

_____

7   The ability to effectively discharge all my financial and accounting responsibilities, including (where this is applicable) financial estimating, costing, budgeting, reporting and controlling; working within estimates; the maintenance of

relevant accounting records and the handling of cash.

I am confident that I fully and effectively discharge such personal responsibilities

\>\>\>\>\>\>

6 5 4 3 2 1

\<\<\<\<\<\<

I fail to effectively discharge such personal responsibilities

Comment_____

_____

Can you think of any training that would improve your competence in this area? Brief comment, please.

_____

_____

A SELF-ASSESSMENT OF YOUR ORGANIZING SKILLS

8 The ability to organize, in general

I consider that I am a consistently excellent organizer

\>\>\>\>\>\>

6 5 4 3 2 1

\<\<\<\<\<\<

I consider that I am a muddled thinker who works without system

Comment_____

_____

Can you think of any training that would improve your organizing ability (e.g. training in forecasting, planning and allocating work; stock planning, purchasing & control; defining objectives and setting standards; project management; personal time management; work analysis; organization and methods; interpretation of plans and data; etc.)? Brief comment, please _____

_____

_____

A SELF-ASSESSMENT OF YOUR COMMUNICATION SKILLS

9   **The ability to communicate verbally with your subordinates in such a manner that understanding and informative feedback is assured.**

I am confident   >>>>>>   I am ineffective
that I put my
points   across   6 5 4 3 2 1
convincingly
and concisely   <<<<<<

Comment_____

_____

_____

10   Written communication

I am confident   >>>>>>   My written work
that my written   is clumsy and
work is always   6 5 4 3 2 1   obscure
cogent, clear &
well set out   <<<<<<

Comment _____

_____

_____

Can you think of any training that would improve your competence in verbal or written communication? Brief comment, please _____

_____

_____

Thank you for completing this self-assessment. If you wish to make any further comment which you consider is relevant to your forthcoming performance review, please do so. _____

_____

_____

_____

_____

_____

Signed _____ Date _____

STAFF CONFIDENTIAL

Name _____

Job Title _____

Dept _____

Appraised by _____

Review Period _____

**PLUNKETTS LTD
STAFF APPRAISAL REPORT**

IMPORTANT Before completing this report, please refer to the pamphlet, 'Notes for Guidance – Completion of the Staff Appraisal Report'. If you are not in possession of this guide, please obtain a copy from the Personnel Manager.

PART A   PERFORMANCE

Overall aspects of performance

1   Job knowledge

Has exceptionally thorough knowledge of all aspects of the job and can apply this knowledge

\>>>>>>

7 6 5 3 2 1

<<<<<<

Is very seriously deficient in all aspects of job knowledge

Comment_____

_____

2   Proficiency in current post

Is oustandingly proficient in all aspects of the job

\>>>>>>

7 6 5 3 2 1

<<<<<<

Incapable of producing acceptable standards of work

Comment_____

_____

3 Resourcefulness as a manager/supervisor

| Is exceptionally resourceful and constructive in his/her approach to the job | >>>>>> 7 6 5 3 2 1 <<<<<< | Is notably lacking in any originality and thought |

Comment_____
_____
_____

4* Ability to organize (see Self-Appraisal Items 1/8)

| Is an outstanding organizer and planner | >>>>>> 7 6 5 3 2 1 <<<<<< | Lacks organizing ability; works without any apparent system |

Comment_____
_____
_____

5* Ability as a leader (see Self-Appraisal, Item 1)

| Is a consistently outstanding and inspiring leader | >>>>>> 7 6 5 3 2 1 <<<<<< | Avoids the responsibilities of leadership at every opportunity |

Comment_____
_____
_____

6   Attendance

Is absent only   >>>>>>   Is often absent
with very good   without   good
reason   6 5 4 3 2 1 reason

<<<<<<

Comment _____

_____

_____

7   Punctuality

Is an exception-   >>>>>>   Is   frequently
al timekeeper   late for work
                   6 5 4 3 2 1 without   good
                              reason
                   <<<<<<

Comment _____

_____

_____

8   Willingness to work overtime

Always   works   >>>>>>   Dislikes   and
excess   hours   shirks overtime
willingly   6 5 4 3 2 1

<<<<<<

Comment _____

_____

_____

Composite rating

_+_+_+_+_+_+_+_= (_)

Specific aspects of performance

9 Competence in delegation

Is exceptionally	>>>>>>	Is a consistently
proficient as a		poor delegator
delegator	6 5 4 3 2 1	

<<<<<<

Comment_____

_____

_____

10* Competence in performance appraisal and counselling of subordinates (see Self-Appraisal, Item 2)

Is exceptionally	>>>>>>	Is incapable of
proficient as an		conducting any
appraiser and	6 5 4 3 2 1	form of apprais-
counsellor		al or counselling

<<<<<<

Comment_____

_____

_____

11* Competence in handling disciplinary and grievance matters (see Self Appraisal, Item 3)

| Is exceptionally competent in the handling of all matters of a disciplinary or grievance nature | >>>>>>
 6 5 4 3 2 1
 <<<<<< | Is incapable of handling any matters of a disciplinary or grievance nature |

Comment _____

_____

_____

12* Non-specialist competence in the identification of subordinates' training needs, implementation or procurement of the training required and the maintenance of training records (see Self-Appraisal, Item 4)

| An exceptionally capable non-specialist trainer | >>>>>>
 6 5 4 3 2 1
 <<<<<< | Is incapable of handling any aspect of his subordinates' training |

Comment _____

_____

_____

13* Competence in the art of positively motivating subordinates (see Self-Appraisal, Item 5)

| Outstanding in every respect as a motivator of employees | >>>>>>
 6 5 4 3 2 1
 <<<<<< | Is incapable of understanding or practising the art of motivation |

Comment _____
_____
_____

14* **Competence in the full and cost-effective utilization of all machinery, equipment and materials within his/her control** (see Self-Appraisal, Item 6)

An exceptional   >>>>>>   Is an incapable
manager of all   manager of all
such resources   6 5 4 3 2 1   such resources

<<<<<<

Comment _____
_____
_____

15* **Competence in relevant financial and/or accounting duties** (see Self-Appraisal, Item 7)

Is outstandingly   >>>>>>   Lacks compe-
competent   in   tence in all such
every respect   6 5 4 3 2 1   duties

<<<<<<

Comment _____
_____
_____

Composite rating

__+__+__+__+__+__+__= (__)

Communication skills

16*   Oral expression (See S/Appraisal Item 9)

Excellent: >>>>>>   Is an ineffective
speaks convin-   speaker
cingly and con- 6 5 4 3 2 1
cisely

           <<<<<<

Comment _____

_____

_____

17*   Written expression (see Staff-Appraisal, Item 10)

Excellent: al-   >>>>>>   Is ineffective;
ways cogent,   written work is
clear and well 6 5 4 3 2 1   very clumsy and
presented   obscure

           <<<<<<

Comment _____

_____

_____

Composite rating

__+__ = (__)

PART B   PERSONAL QUALITIES

18   Sense of duty

Outstanding in every respect: is consistently eager and enthusiastic	>>>>>> 6 5 4 3 2 1 <<<<<<	Invariably places self before duty

Comment_____

_____

_____

19   Judgement

Excellent: his/her proposals and decisions are invariably sound	>>>>>> 6 5 4 3 2 1 <<<<<<	Very poor: is prone to many and varied errors of judgement

Comment_____

_____

_____

20   Reliability under stress

Excellent: he/she is consistently unflustered and competent	>>>>>> 6 5 4 3 2 1 <<<<<<	Very unreliable, even under normal circumstances

Comment_____

_____

_____

21   Co-operation

Excellent: he/   >>>>>>   Totally lacking
she is consis-   in co-operation
tently sensitive 6 5 4 3 2 1 and fails to earn
to the feelings/   the respect of
problems   of   <<<<<<   others
others   and
earns great re-
spect

Comment_____
_____
_____

22   Appearance and bearing

Is exceptionally   >>>>>>   Slovenly in ev-
smart   at   all   ery respect
times – a credit 6 5 4 3 2 1
to his employer
                   <<<<<<

Comment_____
_____
_____

Composite rating

__+__+__+__+__ = (__)

PART C TRAINING RECOMMENDATIONS

_____
_____
_____
_____

PART D RECOMMENDATION FOR PROMOTION

(a) If not recommended for promotion, state reasons

_____

_____

(b) Recommendation for normal promotion:

Recommended ( )   Strongly recommended ( )

Comment _____

_____

_____

(c) Recommendation for special/accelerated promotion

Comment _____

_____

_____

_____

PART E FOR COMPLETION BY APPRAISEE

I have discussed my Self-Appraisal Review and this report with my manager and I have the following comments to make _____

_____

_____

_____

_____

_____

_____

Signature of Apraiser _____ Date _____

Signature of Apraisee _____ Date _____

PART F COUNTERSIGNING MANAGER'S REPORT

_____
_____
_____
_____
_____
_____
_____

Signed _____ Date _____

Appendix 2

ADDITIONAL COPIES OF 'MBO-TYPE' APPRAISAL DOCUMENTATION

STAFF CONFIDENTIAL

Name _____

Job Title _____

Dept _____

Review Period _____

PLUNKETTS LTD
SELF-APPRAISAL REVIEW

NOTES FOR YOUR GUIDANCE

This self-appraisal review is intended to achieve a number of objectives:

(a) to provide a framework for the forthcoming discussion with your manager;

(b) to enable you to assess your overall performance during the period under review;

(c) to enable you to highlight any additional training which you may feel you require in order to perform your job more effectively;

(d) to help you and your manager identify and mutually agree your personal goals during the coming year.

In the event that you have any queries regarding the completion of this review, please do not hesitate to seek the advice of your manager.

PART 1　A REVIEW OF YOUR MAIN JOB RESPONSIBILITIES

Kindly itemize your main job responsibilities, exactly as listed in your current Job Description, and provide an indication of the percentage of working time spent on each one.

Responsibility	% of time

It may well be that you have assumed primary responsibilities that are *not* listed on your Job Description. If so, please itemize these, and provide an indication of the percentage of working time spent on each one.

Responsibility	% of time

PART 2 A REVIEW OF YOUR YEAR'S WORK

What aspect of your year's work do you consider you have done best, or with greatest satisfaction? In your view, how could these strengths be exploited to benefit you and the company?

_____

_____

_____

_____

_____

_____

What do you consider you have done least well, or with least satisfaction? In your view, how could these relative weaknesses be overcome?

_____

_____

_____

_____

_____

_____

It may well have been the case that you were hindered in some aspect(s) of your work by organizational or other problems. If this was so, please

describe the impediments, and suggest how they
could be overcome in the future.

_____

_____

_____

_____

_____

_____

_____

_____

PART 3   IMPROVING YOUR CAPABILITIES

Please consider all the aspects of your job. In your
view, what additional training and/or work experience do you require in order to improve your
capabilities?

_____

_____

_____

_____

After due consideration, you may well feel that
certain organizational/procedural changes (additional to any mentioned by you in Part 2, above),
acquisitions of equipment, etc., would enhance
your capabilities. If so, please describe what you
think is necessary.

_____

_____

_____

_____

_____

PART 4   PLANNING FOR YOUR FUTURE

Please refer to the responsibilities listed by you in Part 1 and, in particular, to those which occupied the bulk of your working time. Bearing in mind that a prime purpose of the forthcoming appraisal discussion is to set your mutually agreed objectives for next year, what do *you* think should be your key goals for the period?

_____
_____
_____
_____
_____
_____
_____
_____
_____
_____

Looking ahead, what do you intend (or hope) to be doing in three to five years' time? How do you see your career developing?

_____
_____
_____
_____
_____
_____
_____
_____

Signed _____   Date _____

STAFF CONFIDENTIAL

Name _____

Job Title _____

Dept _____

Appraised by _____

Review Period _____

PLUNKETTS LTD
STAFF APPRAISAL REPORT

IMPORTANT Before completing this report, please refer to the pamphlet, 'Notes for Guidance – Completion of the Staff Appraisal Report'. If you are not in possession of this guide, please obtain a copy from the Personnel Manager.

PART 1 PERFORMANCE ASSESSMENT

(a) Summary of performance against objectives listed in Part 2 of previous report, including comment on significant achievements related to key tasks.

_____

_____

_____

_____

_____

_____

_____

_____

_____

_____

_____

(b) List specific actions taken since the last performance appraisal to improve the job-holder's capabilities, detailing the improvements achieved.

_____

_____

_____

_____

_____

_____

_____

(c) Performance rating

1 Does not produce an acceptable standard of work

2 Minimally acceptable; requires further training and experience

3 Does not consistently produce a satisfactory standard of performance

4 Achieves a satisfactory standard of performance at all times

5 Has achieved a very high standard of performance at all times

6 Regularly demonstrates outstanding performance

1   2   3   4   5   6

If applicable, indicate specific proposals for improving performance or actioning reassignment.

_____
_____
_____
_____
_____
_____

PART 2   FUTURE PERFORMANCE

List *mutually agreed* performance objectives for the forthcoming period.

_____
_____
_____
_____
_____
_____

_____
_____
_____
_____
_____
_____
_____

Detail any required amendments to the employee's job description.

_____
_____
_____
_____
_____

PART 3 RECOMMENDATION FOR PROMOTION

(a) If not recommended for promotion, state reasons.

_____

(b) Recommendation for normal promotion:

Recommended ( )   Strongly recommended ( )

Comment _____
_____
_____

(c) Recommendation for special/accelerated promotion

Comment _____
_____
_____
_____

PART 4   FOR COMPLETION BY APPRAISEE

I have discussed my Self-Appraisal Review and this report with my manager and I have the following comments to make _____

_____

_____

_____

_____

_____

_____

Signature of Appraiser _____ Date _____

Signature of Appraisee _____ Date _____

PART 5   COUNTERSIGNING MANAGER'S REPORT

_____

_____

_____

_____

_____

_____

Signed _____   Date _____

Recommended reading list

Humble, John, *Management by Objectives in Action*, McGraw-Hill, 1970.

Randell, G., Shaw, R., Packard, P. and Slater, J., *Staff Appraisal*, Institute of Personnel Management, London, 1979.

If you're really keen on collecting views on how long-established appraisal schemes work in practice, have a chat with any and every civil servant, soldier, sailor or airman you come across. Most of 'em are only too pleased to come clean on the subject, even if it does happen to be their pet hate. And if that's construed as an incitement to break the Official Secrets Act, I'd better head for the outback.

Index